# Out of the Jar

**CRAFTED SPIRITS & LIQUEURS**

gestalten

# Contents

WORLD OF
SPIRIT
AND LIQUEUR

 Berries

 Agave

 Grains

 Sugarcane

 Nuts

 Stone Fruit

 Roots & Tubers

 Herbs & Spices

 Pip

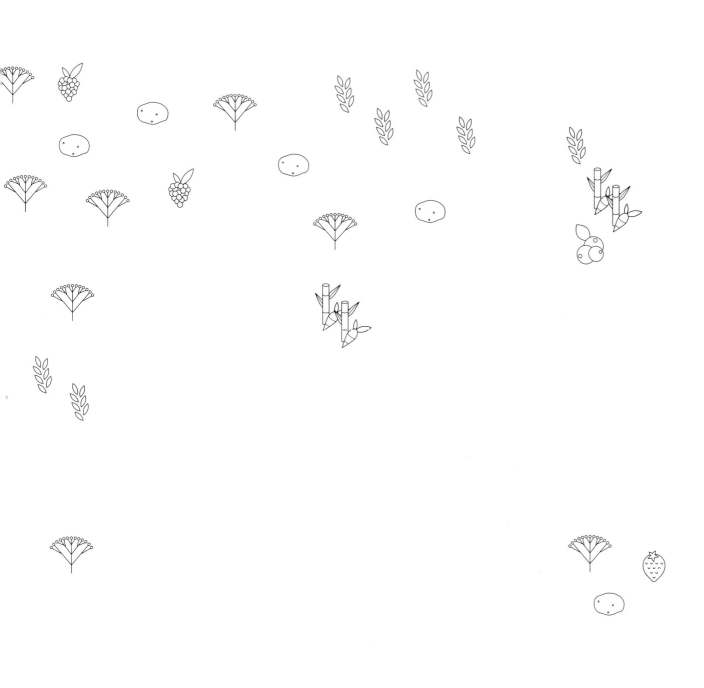

# Foreword

Producing high-strength spirits and liqueurs is an ancient craft that has always been influenced by the nature and culture of the country where it happens. Whether we are talking about whisky from Scotland, cognac from France, rum from the Caribbean, or pisco from Peru, every alcoholic drink is built on a long tradition. What is more, they have all given rise to countless fascinating stories, many of which reach far, far back into the past.

Curiosity for the history of alcohol is a big part of this book. Our main focus, however, is on the here and now, where a refreshing crowd of new and established craftspeople are working in small and medium-sized distilleries to make products that are all defined by:

- an unwavering commitment to natural ingredients,
- a deep love of the craft,
- a fearless desire to experiment,
- an irrepressible enthusiasm for indulgence.

Many new distilleries have opened around the world in recent years. They all aim to preserve the knowledge and skills of the past and reinterpret them for modern times. The combined effect of these newcomers and the distilleries that have been committed to the handcrafted, independent nature of their art for decades has created an extremely dynamic movement. Its members are pioneering, fiercely dedicated to their work, and are breathing new life into an industry dominated by mass-produced, standardized products.

To compile this book, we searched the world over for the most outstanding examples of the craft movement. We discovered extraordinary spirits and liqueurs, and will introduce you to the people who produce them with passion. We have grouped their stories as well as numerous other snapshots of the scene under nine chapters. Like on every great trip there are many things to explore and to learn—and perhaps a surprise or two along the way.

Now all that is left for us to do is wish you a most enjoyable time browsing this guide that we have compiled for all of those who like to seek out and treat themselves to the refined.

Also, please remember to drink responsibly!

# Distillation

•

**It forms the backbone of every spirit: the technique of alcohol distillation has deep roots in our cultural history, with origins in long bygone times. A glimpse back at the development of an artful and elaborate craft.**

The alchemical process of distillation is one of the near-magical discoveries and inventions of our cultural history that continues to fire the human imagination today. Yet we still do not have a complete picture of how distillation evolved over time, and a fair amount of uncharted territory remains on the map. This is all the more surprising if we consider that alcohol very much counts as a staple food in many cultures. In the eighteenth century, for instance, the daily liquor ration for a soldier serving under Frederick the Great in the royal Prussian army was an incredible 0.7 liters! This actually made good sense, as *Branntevin* was extremely high in calories, kept for ages, and was superbly easy to store and transport. It will also have given more than a few infantrymen the extra dose of courage that helped Prussia advance across the bloody battlefields of Europe. And just as it did in Prussia, alcohol has—in rituals, in science, in food supplies, as a drug, and as a source of energy—played its part in our general and cultural development throughout many chapters of human history.

Despite this, alcoholic liquids actually only came about by chance as distillation was evolving (the invention of gunpowder and porcelain, incidentally, also occurred by chance). When people first began experimenting with distillation—about 3,000 years BC—they were not looking to scale new gustatory heights or even find routes into blissful states of intoxication. Theirs was a cosmetic aim: to find a way of trapping fragrances and scents in water. Presumably at the same time as developments were happening in ancient China, people in pre-antiquity Persia were trying to capture the scent of roses and other flowers in liquids. The idea was to make toilet waters, perfumes, and essences that—aside from indulging the senses—would also make it possible to live in a harsh world where human waste and other bodily fluids abounded.

The technique they used was as simple as it was effective. A pot containing a watery mixture—of rose petals, for instance—was put on a fire, and above it would be hung a copper or bronze vessel (or "helmet") that was open at the bottom and had a rim that was folded in on itself. When the rising steam hit the cooler temperature of the helmet, it would condense. The liquid would run off over the rim and could then be collected. This was how the world's first cosmetics were made.

Once fermentation had been discovered—probably by people observing honey ferment in Egyptian clay pots as a forerunner of mead—the way ahead was clear for using distillation techniques (lat. destillare = to drip down) on alcoholic mashes obtained via fermentation. The result was al-kuhul, a very weak alcohol produced in antiquity. It would, however, be a long time before the product was recognized as a drink. Once again, it was primarily used for cosmetic purposes—as a solvent for the "earthly essences" with which people would beautify their faces. Thanks to the arrival of this ancient form of makeup remover, they could now clean the color off. At this stage, alcohol was still a very long way from being fit for consumption and enjoyment.

It was only much later that Persian and Moorish men of science brought distillation, via Sicily and Spain, to Europe. Medieval monasteries and the alchemical laboratories of the Renaissance refined and improved the process. Air cooling, for instance, was replaced by water cooling, which was a first step towards producing stronger alcohols. The next step was double distillation, in which a second round of distillation was used to turn the raw distillate into a spirit with, at the time, an alcohol content of up to 70 percent.

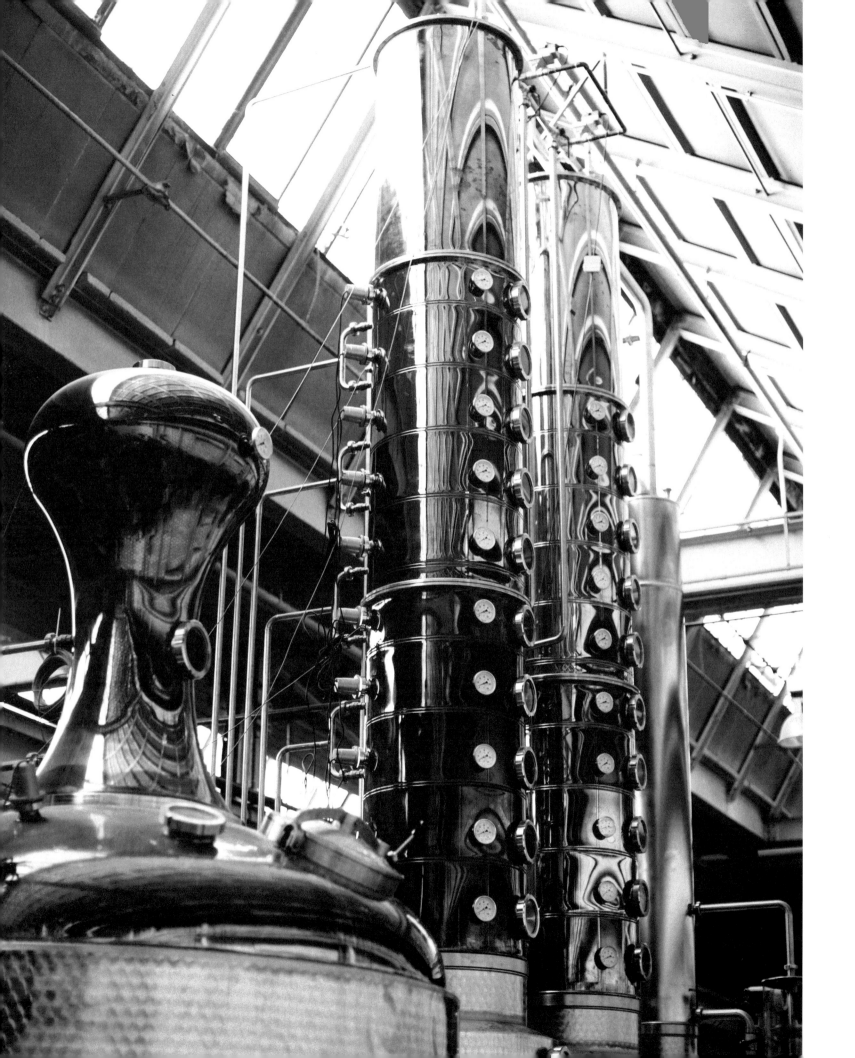

## Burning Water

This stronger alcohol—which was still nowhere near being a drink one could enjoy—presented the people of the Renaissance with a veritable dilemma. They understood their cosmos in terms of the interplay between four clearly distinct elements: water, earth, air, and fire. But now alcohol, or aqua ardens (literally "burning water"), had mixed fire and water, two elements that were believed to be entirely incompatible. The dilemma caused great agitation, inspired hopes for medical breakthroughs, and led to wild speculation. This was the period that gave us two terms we still use today: aqua vitae, or water of life (cf. uisge beatha = whisky in Gaelic) and quinta essentia, the one pure substance that contains the secret of life, the quintessence of nature, or the fifth element. People were seeking the philosopher's stone, and this mysterious liquid promised to be the

solution to every medical problem, a veritable fountain of youth, and the source of life par excellence.

The alcohol of the time was actually a very dirty kind of spirit, full of methanol and oil. This is hardly surprising, given that, obviously, no one knew anything about the byproducts of distillation, the need to separate off the heads and feints, or the structure of alcoholic compounds. And even medicine, if you are expected to drink it, has to taste of something.

Alchemists in the laboratories of monasteries and aristocratic households began to address this issue. They started producing alcohol by fermenting flavorful ingredients (particularly fruit) and adding strong flavors to less palatable (i.e. dirty) alcohol. The first spices to be used in this way, as far back as the thirteenth and fourteenth century, included juniper, wormwood, anise, fennel, and caraway. From today's perspective, it is very easy to see these as first shoots of the family trees of gin/genever, absinthe, aquavit, and anise-based spirits such as ouzo.

## Liquor and Ethanol

These flavorful improvements meant that, during the fifteenth and sixteenth century, alcohol distillation was quietly and with the certainty of making a profit ushered out of the exclusive circle of pharmacists, healers, and doctors, who until then had been the only ones to produce it. Interest among the nobility also helped give rise to early recipes for flavored distillates.

With progressive discoveries concerning the enzymatic breakdown of starches into sugars, it became possible to make alcohol from cheap natural products such as grains or even potatoes. Furthermore, far from being a modern phenomenon, instances of agricultural overproduction were occurring as far back as the early modern period. These two things combined helped bring about the unique case of *Abfindungsbrennereien* (distilleries that qualify for a beneficial tax rate) in the Alpine region of Central Europe.

The development was mainly down to the Habsburgs, led by the distillers' "patron saint", Maria Theresa of Austria. They introduced so-called domestic distilling rights that allowed excess fruit and grains to be processed—with royal approval—in private distilleries in all Habsburg territories. Ever since then, farmers in Hungary, Austria, Switzerland, southern Germany, Spain, northern Italy, eastern France, and the northern parts of the Balkans have been making schnapps on a small scale but in large numbers. It was these thousands of small distilleries that—along with technological advances like Aeneas Coffey's column still and continuous distillation—ensured that the art of distillation became deeply rooted in the traditions, customs, and culinary culture of this region of Central Europe.

Unlike the United States, Britain, France, and Switzerland, few of the countries in Central Europe suffered from any tendencies towards prohibition. This allowed an almost infinite number of the most diverse, regionally specific spirits to flourish. The result is a rich artisanal and culinary heritage that must be preserved for future generations. (Christoph Keller)

## Distillation of Whisky

This diagram shows the production process in a distillery. There are numerous different ways of distilling, each of which produces a different result and volume. In this example, we look at how whiskey is made.

First, the grain, traditionally barley, (1) is malted. Malting involves allowing the grain to germinate so that it converts its starch into sugar (primarily maltose). Heat or hot smoke is used to stop the malting process. After the malt has been ground in a hammer mill (2), it is put into a mash tun (3) and mixed with hot water. This extracts the fermentable sugars contained in the grain. The mash tun has a perforated base that allows the sugar-rich liquid (known as the wort) to run off. The wort is then cooled to about 20 degrees Celsius and pumped into a fermentation tank (4) made of either wood or stainless steel. Yeast is added to start the fermentation process, which converts the sugar into alcohol and carbon dioxide.

After two or three days, this produces an unhopped beer that has an alcohol content of 5 to 8% and is ready to be distilled. The mash is put into a copper still (5) and heated to boiling point. This causes the alcohol to accumulate in the steam and separate off from the liquid. The alcoholic vapor is channeled through the helmet and into the condenser (6), where it is cooled and turned back into a liquid. The raw spirit (low wines) produced by this first distillation is not clean and the alcohol content is too low. It is therefore distilled a second time. This produces the finished spirit that then flows into a spirit safe, which is a small container with an overflow and a hydrometer for measuring the alcohol content. This is where the various cuts (foreshots, heart of the run, and feints) are separated. Only the heart of the run is used. The whiskey is then put into wooden casks (7) and left to age for the desired amount of time. At the end of the maturation process, the whiskey is bottled (8). Water is usually added at this stage to bring the alcohol content down to a drinkable level.

| | | | |
|---|---|---|---|
| 1 | Whisky is made from grain | A | Hammer mill |
| 2 | The grain is ground up | B | Mash tun |
| 3 | The grain is made into a mash | C | Fermentation tank |
| 4 | The mash is fermented | D | Still |
| 5 | Distillation happens in the still | E | Helmet |
| 6 | The alcohol vapors are cooled in the condenser | F | Condenser |
| 7 | The whiskey matures in casks | | |
| 8 | The finished product is bottled | | |

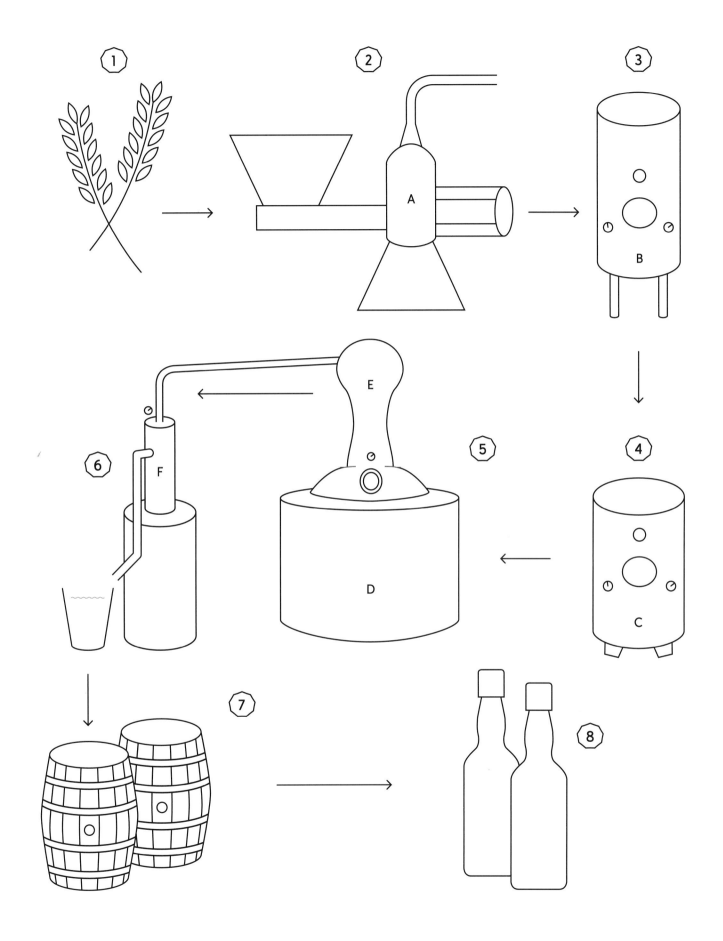

Koval Distillery
18

Glendalough
Distillery
23

Mackmyra Distillery
29

Lark Distillery
27

Whisky Blossoms
in Japan
30

Waiting
for Whiskey
42

Chichibu
Distillery
35

Kings County
Distillery
47

# Water of Life for the World

•

No one knows exactly when Celts in Scotland and Ireland began distilling their *uisge beatha,* or water of life. The details have been lost in the mists of time. However, records from Scottish monasteries suggest the drink had become very popular by the late Middle Ages. Wherever the Celts went, they took their whisky (or whiskey) with them and helped make it popular all over the world.

# Koval Distillery

Just a few years after founding their distillery in Chicago, Sonat and Robert Birnecker had to go looking for new premises. They needed a building that was big enough and, more importantly, had high enough ceilings to accommodate their latest purchase: a copper pot still that stands more than seven meters tall, has two 10-plate distillation columns, and a capacity of 5,000 liters. The dimensions of the still, which was custom-made in Germany, speak volumes about the success of the Koval distillery, which makes gin, vodka, fruit liqueurs, and, above all, whiskey. When Koval opened in 2008 in Chicago—a city better known for beer than spirits—it was the first craft distillery, and indeed the first new distillery, to open in the city for more than a century. In the beginning, a 300-liter still was more than sufficient, but Koval's products soon became extremely popular. That is really not surprising when you know that Austrian-born Robert learned his craft in his grandparents' distillery and brings to the table a level of knowledge and skill that is not all that common in the U.S.

"Prohibition wiped out a lot of knowledge," he says. "Up until a few years ago, classes and further training courses for distillers just didn't exist." These days, Robert teaches at Chicago's Siebel Institute and provides help and advice to those setting up new distilleries.

Koval makes its spirits exclusively from organic grains grown on nearby farms and uses charcoal-filtered water from Lake Michigan. Single grain whiskeys are one of the Birneckers' specialties. In bourbon country, where distillers usually mix several types of grain, these whiskeys are quite the showstoppers. Part of that comes from the fact that Koval uses exotic grains: "We wanted to use varieties of grain that had been neglected. Millet, spelt, and oat mashes were right at the top of our product list. Millet has turned out to be an especially good ingredient, and the customers really like it too," says Robert. Every spirit that comes out of the Koval distillery can be traced back to the cask and on to the organic farmers who supplied the grain.

# KOVAL
# OAT WHISKEY

Distillery · Koval Distillery
Type · Grain Whiskey

Robert Birnecker learned the art of distilling at an early age and quickly joined the distillery run by his Austrian grandfather. Later, when he was working as the deputy press secretary at the Austrian embassy in Washington, he found himself thinking back to his treasured roots and decided to try and make a go of them in America. In 2008, he and his wife Sonat founded Koval Distillery in Chicago—the first to operate within the city limits since prohibition. Their whiskeys, liqueurs, and spirits sell faster than you can blink and have been showered with awards. It did not take long for them to have to upgrade their still from 300 to 5,000 liters. The people of Chicago are particularly taken with Koval's Oat whiskey (40%), which is aged in American oak casks and features notes of caramel and oats.

Alc/Vol: 40%
Location: Chicago (IL), USA
Established: 2008

# KOVAL
# MILLET WHISKEY

Distillery · Koval Distillery
Type · Grain Whiskey

Koval is Chicago's first distillery since the mid-1800s, founded by Robert and Sonat Birnecker upon grain-to-bottle principles. Millet is emblematic of their dedication to the craft as well as innovation: it is the world's first millet whiskey, a grain cultivated in Africa and Asia for thousands of years. Koval source their grain from a local organic farmer collective, mill and mash on site, and distill using a copper pot still handcrafted in Germany by Kothe. The "heart" cut is then aged in new American oak barrels, extracting the full flavor for a unique spirit with a clean finish.

Alc/Vol: 40%
Location: Chicago (IL), USA
Established: 2008

## OLD SUGAR
## QUEEN JENNIE WHISKEY

Distillery · Old Sugar Distillery

Type · Grain Whiskey

Old Sugar Distillery was founded in 2010. Nathan Greenawalt had a still custom-made in the Ozark Mountains and borrowed a truck and trailer to transport it back to Madison. Shortly after that, Wisconsin changed its laws and allowed distilleries to operate tasting rooms. Greenawalt seized the opportunity, and from that point on things just kept getting better. His unusual Queen Jennie whiskey pays homage to Jennie Justo, a bootlegger whose speakeasy kept Madison's residents supplied with liquor during prohibition. Distilled from locally grown millet and aged in small wooden barrels, this gluten-free whiskey tastes like nothing you have ever experienced before.

Alc/Vol: 40%

Location: Madison (WI), USA

Established: 2010

## CORSAIR
## QUINOA WHISKEY

Distillery · Corsair Artisan Distillery

Type · Grain Whiskey

Quinoa, a grain crop grown in Andean communities for thousands of years, has recently found global popularity as a gluten-free, high-protein alternative to other grains. In their search for more imaginative spirits (akin to the broad palette of ingredients used by craft brewers), Nashville-based Corsair Distillery now produces whiskey based on 20% unmalted red and white quinoa seeds in addition to untoasted and toasted varieties of barley. The whiskey, aged in heavily charred American oak barrels, offers a slightly nutty flavor in addition to notes of butter, doughy bread, and dried fruits.

Alc/Vol: 46%

Location: Nashville (TN), USA

Established: 2010

## BRENNE
## FRENCH SINGLE MALT

Distillery · Brenne

Type · Single Malt Whisky

Brenne whisky is still just a baby, really. But although it was only born in 2012, its arrival was preceded by years of planning and testing. Allison and Nital Patel had long been passionate about whisky, but could not find any out-of-the-ordinary distilleries in the United States, where they live. Their successful solution to that problem came about in collaboration with a distiller based in the Cognac region of France. Every step of the whisky-making process—which begins with two well-established varieties of barley as the basic ingredients—happens in France. The highlight of the whisky reveals itself in the ageing process, which lasts roughly seven years. A combination of new Limousin oak casks and used cognac barrels gives the whisky an extremely smooth, creamy structure and an elegantly fruity taste.

Alc/Vol: 40%

Location: Cognac, France

Established: 2012

## GLENDALOUGH
## SINGLE MALT (7 YEARS)

Distillery · Glendalough Distillery
Type · Single Malt Whiskey

Glendalough's five distillers aged their first single malt for seven years. Alongside the picture of St. Kevin, the label features seven crosses that show the location of the Glendalough churches. The distillers say this has nothing to do with lucky numbers: "Here at the Glendalough Distillery, we're not superstitious. We find it brings bad luck." In any case, they treat Ireland's traditions and nature with such care that they are sure to have the support of all the good spirits, forest creatures, and water-dwellers that live in this enchanting valley. In addition to the seven-year-old, which is aged in bourbon barrels and cut to 46% with water from the Wicklow Mountains, the distillery also produces a 13-year-old single malt in the style that first made Irish whiskey great. Its third variety, Double Barrel (42%), is smooth, floral, and aged in bourbon and sherry casks.

Alc/Vol: 46%
Location: Wicklow, Ireland
Established: 2011

## SULLIVANS COVE
## FRENCH OAK

Distillery · Tasmania Distillery
Type · Single Malt Whisky

Sullivans Cove's French Oak, made using only Tasmanian ingredients, was awarded World's Best Single Malt Whisky in 2014—the first whisky outside of Scotland or Japan to claim the honor. Tasmania's whisky tradition began in the early nineteenth century, when Hobart was established as a British penal colony, but in 1838 a total prohibition on distilling would take effect for more than 150 years. Extracting the utmost flavor from Tasmania's rich Franklin barley, French Oak is aged for 12 to 14 years in bourbon and port barrels to achieve a rich palate full of toffee, molasses, and dark chocolate notes.

Alc/Vol: 47,5%
Location: Cambridge, Australia
Established: 1994

# Glendalough Distillery

At the very start of the sixth century, St. Kevin of Glendalough was just a young lad but he had, already started working miracles in his native Ireland. This did not surprise his aristocratic parents as much as you might think, as an angel had told them about their son's special gifts before he was even born. It was, therefore, a foregone conclusion that he would have a religious upbringing in a monastery.

Many years later, when he was returning from a pilgrimage to Rome, he decided to settle in Glendalough, where he built an abbey and lived an ascetic life. With that in mind, it could seem somewhat provocative that Glendalough Distillery features, of all people, the abstinent St. Kevin on the labels of its highly alcoholic products. But as secular as the five young founders of the distillery might appear, they are in fact deeply committed to the traditions of their native country.

Although using St. Kevin as their mascot is a bit cheeky, the distillers point out that is not without reason: "Glendalough was one of the birthplaces of distilling in Ireland. Poitín was first made by Irish monks like St. Kevin. They were the master distillers of their time." The friends, who hail from Wicklow and Dublin, make their gin, whiskey, and poitín surrounded by the unspoiled nature of Glendalough, which lies 50 kilometers south of the capital.

Traditional poitín has always been made from malted barley, sugar beet, and potatoes. The drink was banned in the seventeenth century, supposedly because it fueled the rebellious spirit of the Irish, and had to be made in secret for centuries thereafter. When the Glendalough distillers put their first poitín on the market, they needed to prove that they could handle the ancient Irish tradition with the respect it deserves. And although they give their poitíns a unique character, the results are absolutely in keeping with their Glendalough legacy.

## SLYRS
## SINGLE MALT WHISKY

Distillery · Slyrs Destillerie
Type · Single Malt Whisky

This spirit started over a wager in Scotland: Florian Stetter bet that he would create a single malt whisky in his native Upper Bavaria. Upon his return, he concentrated the distilling and aging process in a new distillery in Neuhaus. The barley malt is sourced from lower altitudes in nearby Bamberg and milled at SLYRS, then fermented using alpine spring water for seven days and finally distilled in distinctive stills with bow-shaped lyne arms. After maturing for three years in barrels of virgin American white oak, the unpeated whisky acquires pleasantly malty and woody notes and fruity aromas.

Alc/Vol: 43%
Location: Schliersee, Germany
Established: 1999

## COTSWOLDS
## SINGLE MALT WHISKY

Distillery · The Cotswolds Distillery
Type · Single Malt Whisky

Inspired by the abundant barley fields planted over the rolling hills of the Cotswolds, native New Yorker Dan Szor set out to make the region's first single malt whisky. He transformed an old barn into a fully-functioning distillery with copper batch pot stills from Forsyths, and assembled a team of specialists, including a botanist and wood-ageing consultant, for an entirely local process of growing, harvesting, malting, mashing, and distilling. The whisky, aged in bourbon, sherry, and wine casks for three years, has a rich, fruity depth, reflecting the unique terroir of the Cotswolds.

Alc/Vol: 46%
Location: Stourton, United Kingdom
Established: 2014

## THE BELGIAN OWL
## SINGLE MALT WHISKY

Distillery · The Owl Distillery
Type · Single Malt Whisky

The Belgian Owl is entirely Belgian, from cultivation to bottling, using local groundwater and practicing fair trade and eco-friendly methods in the Goreux farmlands. Working with Pierre Roberti, a seventh-generation farmer, they grow a particular Belgian barley that produces the distinctive taste of their single malt whisky. Drawing on his education at Bruichladdich Distillery in Scotland, Etienne Bouillon oversees the whisky purification in two century-old pot stills from Caperdonich Distillery, followed by three years of aging in first-filled bourbon casks from Heaven Hill Distillery.

Alc/Vol: 46%
Location: Fexhe-le-Haut-Clocher, Belgium
Established: 2004

# SPRINGBANK
## SPRINGBANK (21 YEARS)

Distillery · Springbank Distillers
Type · Single Malt Whisky

The area around Campbeltown on Scotland's Kintyre peninsula has been involved in whisky production for as long as anyone can remember. The first written record of Campbeltown whisky dates back to 1591. At that time, the isolated coastal town had everything it needed to become a center of whisky smuggling. Even the Mitchell family was involved in illegal distilling before it opened a legitimate company in the form of Springbank Distillers. Many of the production processes and some of the buildings date back to Victorian times, and the single malts are kept deliberately old fashioned. The distillery also does its own floor malting by hand. The Springbank 21-year-old is made from a recipe that comes from the very early days of the distillery. The result is a creamy dram with notes of strawberry and hints of sugared almonds.

Alc/Vol: 46 %
Location: Campbeltown, United Kingdom
Established: 1828

# SPRINGBANK
## CASK STRENGTH (12 YEARS)

Distillery · Springbank Distillers
Type · Single Malt Whisky

In 2013, a Chinese collector bought a 50-year-old Springbank whisky for 68,000 Euros. Imagine what the stereotypical thrifty Scot would think about that! In any case, the sale was clearly a big deal for Springbank Distillers, and it now features on the timeline of the family's story. Its history stretches right back to the seventeenth century, when the first Mitchells were working as maltsters in the area around Campbeltown. Archibald Mitchell was the first distiller in the family, which got a license for its own whisky distillery in 1828. The Springbank 12-year-old is a comparatively young single malt. Aged under the watchful eye of Archibald's great-great grandson and bottled at cask strength, it is alive with flavors of raisin, fig, linseed oil, and just a touch of papaya. Adding a drop of water is said to release warm milk chocolate and vanilla notes.

Alc/Vol: 54.3 %
Location: Campbeltown, United Kingdom
Established: 1828

| PEATED | URANIA | LARK SINGLE MALT WHISKY |
|---|---|---|

Distillery · Stauning Whisky
Type · Single Malt Whiskey

Distillery · Spirit of Hven
Type · Single Malt Whisky

Distillery · Lark Distillery
Type · Single Malt Whisky

Stauning Whisky has its roots in a weekend break, when a group of friends—all male, all somewhere between 30 and late 50s—realized it was odd that no one was making whisky in Denmark. Nine pairs of eyes started to shine at the idea of doing something about this in their spare time. And so Denmark's first whisky team was made up of four engineers, a pilot, a butcher, a chef, a doctor, and a teacher running a distillery housed in a former butcher's shop. To make their Peated whisky, the Stauning men malt the Danish barley themselves and dry the grains over peat smoke. The twice-distilled spirit spends three years in bourbon casks and, despite its youth, delivers a mature flavor that brings to mind smoky chocolate, nougat, and molasses. Peated won gold at the 2013 International Review of Spirits Competition.

Back in the 16th century, astronomer Tycho Braha named the observatory he erected here after the Greek muse Urania, bringing worldwide renown to this small Swedish island with only four villages. Because her dedication brought such good luck in the past, it only made sense that she should pass some of it on to Urania Single Malt, produced by the local distillery Spirit of Hven. She has an influence on the stars, which make the barley on Hven flourish, create an ideal ratio of minerals and salt in the water, and aid in the dispersal of three sensitive yeast variations. Beyond these three ingredients—and the muse's good graces, of course—nothing more is required to make this fresh, peppery single malt, which is aged for three years in triple-oak barrels.

"I wonder why there isn't anyone making malt whisky in Tasmania," said Bill Lark to his father-in-law Max as they shared a dram or two on a trout fishing trip. Perhaps Bill was hoping that Max would tell him to give it a go, but that kind of whisky undertaking should not be built on doubts. In the end, Bill did the right thing and founded Lark Distillery in 1992. In doing so, he put Tasmania's ideal whisky climate, its fields of barley, highland peat bogs, and wonderfully soft water to good use. The Lark Single Malt Whisky (43%), which is made from Tasmanian barley, is the distillery's flagship product. Aged in small, 100-liter casks for up to eight years, it starts out with floral, fruity aromas and then ushers in hints of plum pudding and malt before finishing with a delicate suggestion of highland peat.

Alc/Vol: 55%
Location: Stauning, Denmark
Established: 2005

Alc/Vol: 45%
Location: Sankt Ibb, Sweden
Established: 2008

Alc/Vol: 43%
Location: Hobart, Tasmania, Australia
Established: 1992

# Lark Distillery

If you ever find yourself daydreaming about Australia, your imaginary landscapes probably do not include highland peat bogs. Yet if you were to travel to Tasmania, which lies some 240 kilometers off the south coast of Australia, you would actually find some. So it is only those who are unfamiliar with the place who are surprised to learn that this far-away island produces European-style whiskies. (Interesting side note: Tasmania is almost exactly the same size as Ireland.) Whisky fans living down under had to first weather a bit of a drought, though. Some 150 years separate the closing of Tasmania's last distillery and Bill Lark deciding in 1992 to take the plunge and fill the supply gap. The idea came about during a fishing trip that Bill took with his father-in-law Max. While the two men enjoyed a glass of the single malt that Max had brought along, they realized that Tasmania had the ideal conditions for making premium whisky. It had fields of barley, peat bogs, and extremely soft, pure water from the island's rainforests. Another gift from the whisky gods was that Bill's wife Lyn and daughter Kristy proved excellent at distinguishing the flavors in the spirit. Both women have bucked the male-dominated trend in the industry by becoming master distillers for the family-run company. Small cask ageing is another of the distillery's trademarks. Compared to large barrels, small casks provide a higher ratio of wood surface area to volume of liquid, which means they have a greater impact on the flavor. This is probably one reason why this boutique-style whisky has won so many awards in the Old World and cemented Tasmania in the minds of whisky connoisseurs everywhere.

## MCCARTHY'S OREGON SINGLE MALT WHISKEY

Distillery · Clear Creek Distillery
Type · Single Malt Whiskey

Stephen McCarthy launched his Oregon single malt whiskey at the cusp of its comeback in the American palate, and has maintained its exceptional quality for several decades. Made in the Islay tradition, peat-malted barley from Scotland's Port Ellen distillery is imported and distilled in Clear Creek's Holstein pot stills in a single pass, then aged in air-dried Oregon oak barrels for at least three years. The award-winning result is a very peaty whiskey, reminiscent of pine, oak, and the gentle sweetness of barley, with an aroma comparable to Islay single malt scotches aged for far longer.

Alc/Vol: 40%
Location: Portland (OR), USA
Established: 1985

## KILCHOMAN SINGLE MALT MACHIR BAY

Distillery · Kilchoman Distillery
Type · Single Malt Whisky

Anthony Wills is clearly a talented father. How else could he have gotten his three sons (George, Peter, and James) so productively involved in his whisky distillery from the very start? In 2005, the year it was founded on the Scottish island of Islay, the brothers would try to outdo each other at sweeping, cleaning, and polishing. These days, they handle the company's sales and marketing operations. The Kilchoman Distillery is the first new distillery to open on Islay (also known as the Queen of the Hebrides) in more than a century. From the outset, Wills wanted to grow his own barley on the neighboring farm and malt it himself. Those are tough jobs, but it has been well worth the effort. Machir Bay single malt won gold at the IWSC the very first year it went on sale. Aged in bourbon and sherry casks, the whisky has aromas of tropical fruit, peat, and vanilla, and rounds them off with a wonderfully intense sweetness.

Alc/Vol: 46%
Location: Islay, United Kingdom
Established: 2005

## MACKMYRA BRUKSWHISKY

Distillery · Mackmyra Distillery
Type · Single Malt Whisky

This sounds very much like something you "have to do" once you have ticked off a house, a family, and all the other milestones: Swedish whisky company Mackmyra will allow you to configure your own personal cask, have it fitted with a nameplate, and put away to age. While you are waiting for the whisky to mature (which will take at least three years), you can entertain yourself with a bottle of Mackmyra's Brukswhisky. Aged in bourbon, sherry, and Swedish oak casks, this peppery, fruity single malt has aromas of butter toffee, pear, licorice, and citrus fruits. It also won gold at the IWSC in 2010. The Mackmyra story began back in 1999, when eight friends founded Sweden's first whisky distillery. Their products benefit from the country's pure water, the slow-growing, spicy oak that makes their casks, and the barley that owes its distinctive sweetness to the long summer days.

Alc/Vol: 41.4%
Location: Gävle, Sweden
Established: 1999

# Mackmyra Distillery

In the winter of 1998, a group of Swedish friends went skiing. One evening, when they were relaxing over a glass or two of Scottish whisky, a question came up that no one could answer: "Why are there no whisky distilleries in Sweden?" After doing some research, they learned that Sweden actually has everything a whisky industry needs: an abundance of pure spring water, good barley growing in the fields, and even oak trees for the casks.

The country was only distillery-free because no one had ever had the idea of opening one. That has all changed now. Sweden has grown from being a country of whisky drinkers to a country of whisky makers. Mackmyra, the distillery founded by the eight skiers in 1999, has played a leading role in this development. A lot has happened since they filled their first 30-liter cask back in 2000. Angela D'Orazio, Mackmyra's master blender, still gets a kick out of remembering how, when her Preludium 01 whisky went on sale in 2007, the 4,000 bottles sold out in less than an hour. The distillery has since won several international awards, including European Whisky of the Year and European Spirits Producer of the Year. Mackmyra is named after the place where it was founded. All the ingredients, including the water, peat, and yeast, come from nearby. The casks are stored 50 meters underground in a disused mine. Most of the whiskies are bottled at cask strength. Mackmyra's success has stirred up Sweden's spirits and bar scene, and has inspired many others to open their own distilleries. These days, no one has any cause to wonder why Sweden has no whisky industry.

# Whisky Blossoms in Japan

•

**The delicate bud of Japanese whiskey production at the beginning of the 20th century initially went unnoticed, even in its own land. But after a bit of early frost damage, it is now in full bloom.**

A famous scene from *Lost in Translation* sees Bill Murray filming an advertisement for Japanese whisky. For many, this was the first they had heard of a whisky industry in Japan. What a lot of people do not know is that the country is the third biggest whisky producer in the world, after Scotland and the U.S. and before Ireland. The myths surrounding the beginnings of Japan's two oldest whisky distilleries center on the lives of two men, Masataka Taketsuru and Shinjiro Torii, the fathers of Japanese whisky.

Masataka Taketsuru was born in 1894 as the heir to a sake dynasty. He began studying chemistry at Osaka's technical university in 1916. The idea was that, once he had graduated, he would take over and modernize the family business. However, things did not work out that way. During his studies, the young Taketsuru became fascinated with spirits from the West. He was especially taken with whisky. In 1854, a previously isolated Japan had opened up to the world and started importing whisky, first from the U.S., then from Scotland. The early twentieth century saw it become a popular drink in the busy hotel bars of Tokyo, Nagasaki, and Osaka. This was the point in time that Japanese companies began thinking seriously about starting their own whisky industry. Settsu Shuzo, a spirits company based in Osaka, leaped into action when the First World War ended and sent Taketsuru to Glasgow in late 1918. His task: to uncover the secrets of whisky-making and bring them back to Japan. Once again, though, things did not go as planned. When Taketsuru returned home in 1920, he brought more than just his newly acquired whisky expertise with him. Although both families were heavily opposed to it, his Scottish bride, Jessie Roberta "Rita" Cowan accompanied him. Meanwhile, the postwar recession had forced Settsu Shuzo to shelve its whisky plans. This, combined with the fact that the Taketsuru clan were outraged by the wedding, meant the newlyweds had to earn their crust as teachers for a while.

As all this was happening, Shinjiro Torii, who also hailed from Osaka, was keeping himself busy. In 1899, following an apprenticeship as a wine and spirits merchant, Torii, then barely 20 years old, started his first company, Torii Shoten, and tried his hand at making liqueurs. His sweet spirits were to the Japanese people's liking. Within two decades, he grew his small spirits business into Kotobukiya Limited. In 1923, he caused an extremely lucrative scandal when he ran Japan's first erotic advertising campaign. All the while, Torii was dreaming about opening Japan's first whisky distillery. Against the wishes and advice of his investors and directors, he began looking for a suitable location and a whisky expert. He was successful on both counts. The location was Yamazaki, which was close to a source of pure spring water and not far from Kyoto. The expert was Masataka Taketsuru.

And so it was, that in 1924 the fathers of Japanese whisky embarked on their 10-year collaboration. It soon became clear, however, that the two men had very different ideas about the kind of whisky that should be produced in Yamazaki. In 1929, after five long years of waiting, Taketsuru brought the distillery's first whisky, Shirofuda, to the market. The product reflected the master distiller's Scottish influences, but its heavy, smoky flavor was too much for the Japanese, who were used to sweeter tastes. They did not like Shirofuda—and neither did Torii, since its failure posed a risk to his considerable investments. He demanded that Taketsuru make a more likeable whisky. When Taketsuru stubbornly refused to give up his Scottish ideals, Torii wasted no time in transferring him to one of Kotobukiya Limited's breweries. The 10-year contract between Taketsuru and Torii's company ended in 1934. And while Torii was already busy developing a blended whisky that would meet his needs, Taketsuru, with the support of his wife Rita, returned to his dream of making Scottish whisky in Japan.

Shinjiro Torii, the founder of Suntory, created a Japanese whisky adapted to Japanese tastes.

On a visit to Japan's northern Hokkaido island, he found climatic conditions that reminded him of Scotland. Taketsuru thus chose to set up his own company there in 1934. He called it Nippon Kaju K.K., though the name would later change to Nikka. Things were tough for the Taketsurus over the next few years until the first batch of Nikka whisky was ready for bottling in 1940. Torii, meanwhile, had launched his Suntory Kakubin in the iconic tortoise-shell bottle in 1937 and was celebrating his first successes.

In the end, the lasting success and economic stability of both whisky producers was secured by a single event that no one could have predicted: the Second World War. Japanese soldiers drank so much whisky in the 1940s that the government classed Kotobukiya and Nikka as being crucial to the war effort and made them a priority for supplies. When the war ended, the soldiers returned home and carried on drinking their whisky. The Scottish spirit had finally gotten a foothold in Japan, and when its popularity exploded in

the 1960s and 1970s, both companies profited. In 1963, with the launch of Suntory beer—the first of many successful forays into other markets—Kotobukiya permanently changed its name to Suntory. Nikka and Suntory continue to rule the Japanese whisky market today and have achieved the same global-player status enjoyed by many Scottish and U.S. brands.

「人間」らしく
やりたいナ

トリスを飲んで
「人間」らしく
やりたいナ

「人間」なんだからナ

サントリー姉妹品

**トリスウィスキー**

●大瓶330円　●ポケット瓶120円　●デラックス500円

## ON THE WAY

Distillery · Chichibu Distillery
Type · Single Malt Whisky

On the Way, a single malt from Japan's Chichibu distillery, has a name that gets you thinking. Does it perhaps refer to the fact that the whisky takes a tour of several different casks before it reaches the bottle? Distiller Ichiro Akuto begins by letting it age in two different bourbon oak casks from his own The Floor Malted. He then transfers it to a mizunara cask from a 2008 whisky, where it stays until it has aged a full five years. The distillery lies to the northwest of Tokyo, nestled in the beautiful hills around Chichibu. Akuto and the single malts he produces there have picked up where his father failed to turn a profit. His whiskies have won numerous awards and have attracted a cult following.

Alc/Vol: 58.5%
Location: Chichibu, Japan
Established: 2008

## CHIBIDARU 2014

Distillery · Chichibu Distillery
Type · Single Malt Whisky

Jim Murray's recent decision to name a Yamazaki the best whisky in the world has caused demand for Japanese grain spirits to reach unprecedented levels. This is very good news for Ichiro Akuto, who has been tirelessly producing whisky in his Chichibu distillery since 2008. Akuto distils his barley in a small still, skips the cold filtration step, and leaves the results to mature in various types of casks. Tracking down world-class whiskies in the Land of the Rising Sun is pretty easy—a fact that must surely have instilled itself in the minds of Western drinkers by now.

Alc/Vol: 53.5%
Location: Chichibu, Japan
Established: 2008

## CHIBIDARU

Distillery · Chichibu Distillery
Type · Single Malt Whisky

Japanese distiller Ichiro Akuto is not a pedant. The reason his Chibidaru whisky has a rather awkward ABV figure is because the single malt is bottled at cask strength. Not a single drop of water is added for the sake of a rounder number. What is more, natural variations in alcohol content mean the figure changes depending on the year the whisky was bottled. The batch that emerged from the 150-liter, shortened hogshead casks in 2014 registered a golden 53.5% on the ABV scale. This Chibidaru is big, floral, and fresh, with aromas of fig and melon. On the palate, it brings to mind cocoa beans, coconuts, and a pinch of salt. The finish is long and elegant with shades of almond and saffron.

Alc/Vol: 53.5%
Location: Chichibu, Japan
Established: 2008

# Chichibu Distillery

Ichiro Akuto's story is a good one. Like all good stories, his tells of dreams and acts of bravery, of family and traditions, of failures and triumphs. And although the tale does not yet have an ending, it is certainly on a very happy path.

The Akuto family had been producing traditional sake in Chichibu for more than 300 years when, in 1941, Ichiro's grand-father opened a second distillery in nearby Hanyu. His son began producing Scottish-style whisky there in the 1980s. Un-fortunately, this was at a time when highballs and blended whiskies were all the rage and Japan was not yet ready for single malts. In 2000, the Hanyu site was up for sale and Ichiro Akuto, the heir to the family business, was watching his dreams of a flourishing distillery evaporate. But when the buyers decided to put the stocks of Hanyu whisky up for sale, Akuto enlisted the help of investors, bought 400 casks, and started his own company, Venture Whisky Ltd. What came next sparked a veritable frenzy among whisky lovers and collectors, and has probably changed the Japanese whisky market forever.

Akuto gradually bottled the Hanyu whisky and put it on the market in limited editions that were named after playing cards. The Joker, the last batch of the now-legendary card collection, featured a vatting of six Hanyu whiskies spanning the period from 1985 to 2000. Almost as soon as the 400 casks of Hanyu whisky were empty, Akuto started replenishing his stocks. In 2007, he founded the Chichibu Distillery and started bottling his first whisky, Newborn, in 2009. He christened his first five-year-old whisky On The Way. Both whiskies were well received by con-noisseurs and critics alike. All of a sudden, the Japanese whisky market, which has traditionally been dominated by industry giants Suntory and Nikka, is being well and truly shaken up. Emboldened by Chichibu's success and the international attention it is receiving, new artisan whisky distilleries have begun popping up all over Japan. And Ichiro Akuto is continuing to work on the next chapter of his story.

# TEELING WHISKEY
# IRISH WHISKEY

Distillery · Teeling Whiskey Co.
Type · Blended Whiskey

Walter Teeling opened the first Teeling family distillery in 1782. At the time, he was one of 37 Dublin distillers who secured Irish whiskey an excellent reputation throughout the world. But as the years went by, things got tough. The lowest point of all came in 1976, when Dublin's last distillery was forced to throw in the towel. But now Stephen and Jack Teeling are in the prime of life and ready to try for a new beginning. The weight of expectation might be heavy, but they have a wealth of experience and a large stock of family whiskey on which to draw. In collaboration with micro-distiller Alex Chasko, the brothers want to revive the tradition while tastefully stirring it up. Their flagship Small Batch is a blended whiskey aged in rum casks and bottled at a robust 46%. It features sweet, spicy, and slightly woody notes.

Alc/Vol: 46%
Location: Dublin, Ireland
Established: 2012

# SNAKE RIVER STAMPEDE

Distillery · Indio Spirits
Type · Blended Whiskey

Snake River Stampede begins its life as Canadian grain, a custom blend of rye with corn and barley. The distillate is aged in bourbon barrels for up to eight years and finished with an additional six months in sherry barrels to unite the flavors. The result is finally bottled by Indio Spirits near Portland, Oregon, although the whiskey's namesake comes from the century-old rodeo in Idaho—indeed, the presidents of the rodeo and the distillery came up with the idea as seat-mates on an airplane. Snake River Stampede is redolent with dusty rye, giving way to ginger, white pepper, and dark fruits.

Alc/Vol: 40%
Location: Portland (OR), USA
Established: 2006

# Waiting for Whiskey

•

The market for handcrafted whiskey is booming. Each year sees a rise in the number of small and micro distilleries being set up around the world. However, depending on a country's regulations and the distiller's aspirations, it can be a good few years before the first batch of whiskey comes out of storage and goes on sale. Surviving this period is a financial challenge for new distilleries everywhere.

A lot of the new distilleries are set up by whiskey fans moving into the industry from another career. The success of Sweden's Mackmyra distillery is attracting increasing international attention. It is not unusual for a start-up to begin with a whole group of friends who, after spending an evening drinking whiskey together, decide to try and make the first or the best whiskey in their country. "It must be possible!" they say, and many do go on to take that brave step. In most cases, the founders build up their companies on the basis of learning by doing. Each distillery develops its own plan as to how it will survive the period before it can start bottling. Some of the most successful strategies are in use in start-up distilleries around the world.

One of those strategies involves a spirit like gin. While the freshly distilled whiskey spends the required or desired amount of time aging in wood casks, the distillery produces and sells a spirit that does not need to mature. The most common choice in Europe is gin, while moonshine or white whiskey are popular in the U.S.

The first distillery to open in Helsinki in over a century, for instance, is filling the three years that its regional rye whiskey will

spend in French casks by distilling gin from Finnish juniper and making applejack from native apple varieties.

Its "neighboring" distillery, Myken, lies on a small Norwegian island in the Arctic Circle. Housed in an old fish factory, the distillery recently became home to three handmade copper stills from Spain. It will probably be quite a while before the five couples who founded the company are able to live from the profits. In the meantime, they too are planning to make very Nordic gin. They are also thinking about opening a restaurant on the top floor of the factory. Their target market includes tourists, sailors, and, of course, visitors to what is currently Norway's most northerly distillery.

Another good way of bridging the gap until your own whiskey is ready is to buy and bottle a different whiskey. In these cases, it is important that buyers know what they are getting and that the product has a good story behind it. Ichiro Akuto, the founder of Japan's Chichibu distillery, had a particularly good tale to tell. He earned himself a cult following after he started bottling and selling the whisky he bought from the insolvent estate of his grandfather's company.

Yet another popular source of income involves pre-selling the first few bottles or even whole casks. The Milk & Honey Distillery in Tel Aviv is planning to bring the art of distilling back to the Middle East by producing a premium whiskey in the Holy Land. It is set to go on sale in 2017. The founders have supplemented their seed capital by pre-selling bottles and launching a crowdfunding campaign.

The London Distillery Company is the first whiskey distillery to open in the city since 1903. Its three founders are selling a limited edition of small bourbon casks as a way of increasing the anticipation and shortening the wait for their whiskey.

# Kings County Distillery

David Haskell and Colin Spoelman of Kings County Distillery could claim to run what is both the oldest and the youngest whiskey-making outfit in New York City. In 2008, they became the first to receive a distillery license from the New York State Liquor Authority, which probably makes them the first distillers to operate legally in New York since prohibition ended.

Since then, more than 800 casks have taken up residence in Kings County Distillery, which occupies an old brick building on the Brooklyn Navy Yard. This is where Haskell and Spoelman make their moonshine, bourbon, and chocolate whiskey, which they sell in 375-milliliter bottles with a sleek, minimalist design. They produce about 40 of their 20-liter casks and a few 50-liter casks every month. Most of those stay put to age on the premises.

The Kings County story begins back in 2007, when Haskell and Spoelman, who knew each other from Yale, decided to order a small still online. Kentucky-born Spoelman had previously brought back a gallon of moonshine from home, which made the pair wonder whether they could make their own whiskey. "The first batches were pretty bad," says Spoelman, "but we wanted to learn and prove that you can make unaged whiskey that is actually quite interesting and drinkable." As the results improved and Kings County made a name for itself, Haskell and Spoelman decided to stop distilling in their apartment and start doing things the legal way. Luckily for them, the New York authorities had just decided to significantly reduce the cost of licenses for small distilleries. And so the pair became business partners—and pioneers of what is now a burgeoning craft distillery scene in New York City.

# STRANAHAN'S
# COLORADO WHISKEY

Distillery · Stranahan's Colorado Whiskey
Type · American Malt Whiskey

When Jess Graber, a volunteer firefighter, was called out to tackle a blaze at George Stranahan's shed, the two got to talking about their shared passion for whiskey. Despite the dicey situation that gave rise to it, their plan to set up Colorado's first micro distillery was not a heat-of-the-moment idea. They opened Stranahan's Colorado Whiskey in Denver in 2004 and began making whiskey using water and barley from the Rocky Mountains. Every three weeks, they select 10 to 20 barrels and combine them to produce a small batch—enough for about 5,000 bottles. Anyone who wants to be part of the volunteer Bottling Crew can register online via the website. Helpers have to work for five hours, but the time passes quickly and is apparently rewarded with a bottle of Stranahan's whiskey. The waiting list, however, is rumored to have about 20,000 names on it already.

Alc/Vol: 47%
Location: Nashville (TN), USA
Established: 2004

# KINGS COUNTY
# BOURBON WHISKEY

Distillery · Kings County Distillery
Type · Bourbon Whiskey

When Kings County Distillery opened in East Williamsburg, New York, in 2010, it was the smallest commercial distillery in the United States and made its whiskey in five 24-liter stainless steel stills. In 2012, it moved to the historic Brooklyn Navy Yard and acquired some gigantic Scottish-made copper stills. These are responsible for producing, among other things, the distillery's bourbon whiskey. Made from organic New York corn and British malted barley, the bourbon is aged in American oak charred barrels and delivers rich aromas of corn followed by sweet vanilla and caramel with a twist of autumn spices. Aged a minimum of just 12 months, this is a full-fledged, robust whiskey that featured in Eric Asimov's top ten bourbons for the *New York Times.*

Alc/Vol: 45%
Location: New York (NY), USA
Established: 2010

Potocki Vodka
53

Bottled Spuds
56

Mikkeller Brewery
62

# Crystal Clear

•

While Korn is always a grain spirit, generally made from wheat, barley, or rye, most countries have no rules about what the basic ingredient of vodka should be. Surplus harvests in the nineteenth century led Poland and Ukraine to start making vodka from potatoes. Unlike Korn, vodka is heavily filtered to achieve the neutral taste that is considered the ultimate mark of quality.

# POTOCKI WODKA

Distillery · Potocki Spirits
Type · Grain vodka

In a category of spirits where producers like to define their products by how often they have been distilled, a vodka that only goes through the process twice has found a pleasing way to set itself apart from the crowd. When the distiller goes even further and opts out of using filtration methods that downsize the taste, you know that you are dealing with a true Polish family recipe. This rye vodka is the kind that the Potocki family were making between 1816 and 1944, and has very little in common with the industrially produced vodkas that you normally find doing the rounds.

Alc/Vol: 40%
Location: Region Wielkopolska Poland
Established: 1816

# KOZUBA STARKUS

Distillery · Z. Kozuba i Synowie
Type · Grain vodka

If you ask the three Kozuba brothers where their new Starkus vodka comes from, chances are they will tell you the stork brings it. Tales of storks delivering newborns have particularly long roots in a country as staunchly Catholic as Poland. The Kozubas actually make their barrel-aged rye vodka themselves, far out in the countryside and in small batches. They use rye that grows nearby, malt it, ferment it, and then distill it in their copper still. The vodka gets its amber color from being stored in American white oak casks after they have been used for ageing rye whiskey. This kind of vodka is known as starkus (stork) vodka because of an old custom: whenever a baby was born, the man of the house would bury a barrel of homemade vodka in anticipation of the child's wedding day.

Alc/Vol: 40%
Location: Jabłonka, Poland
Established: 2005

# Potocki Wodka

When Poles hear the name Potocki, they feel a deep sense of pride. This aristocratic family and its many branches have produced countless statesmen, authors, and the name of an archipelago in the Yellow Sea, which was named after Jan Potocki. But it is not just the men who have made names for themselves: Delfina Potocka could pride herself on being the muse of the great composer Frédéric Chopin. These days, a vodka from the House of Potocki is attracting a great deal of attention—little wonder, since the spirit is in the family's blood.

After a forced break of nearly 60 years (the Communists nationalized Lancut Palace and its eighteenth-century vodka distillery in 1944), the vodka tradition has been revived by Jan-Roman Potocki, who makes it using rye that he grows in fields near the distillery. When harvest time rolls around in August, the fresh grains are quickly mixed with yeast and processed to produce the mash. After that, the brakes go on. Two slow distillations raise the alcohol content to 96%, after which water is added to bring it down to a more drinkable 40%. The usual charcoal filtration is deliberately omitted so as to retain the vodka's characteristic taste. Good vodka, says Potocki, should keep the palate entertained for 30 seconds. His vodka starts out soft and slightly sweet, allows the rye's nutty flavors to come to the fore, and then leaves you with a warm glow in your heart. The Russians say it is too mellow, but Potocki Vodka has become a fixture in chic bars and restaurants in China, the U.S., and Western Europe.

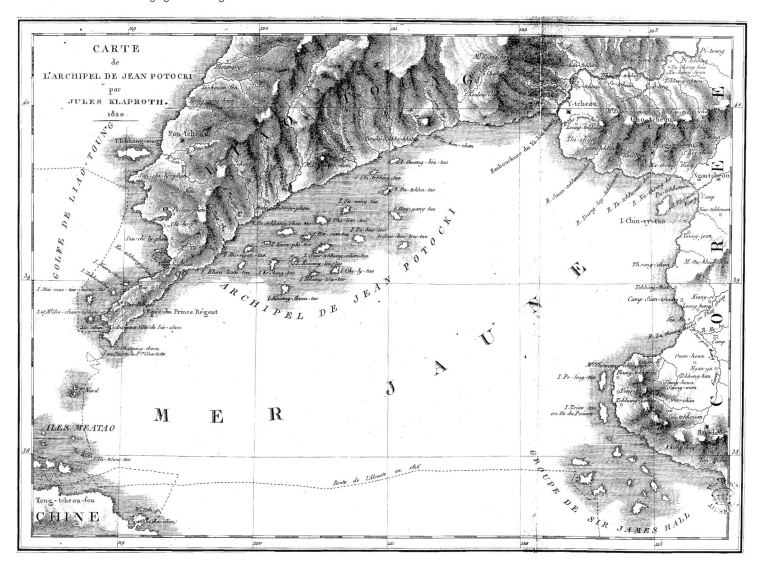

## IRONWORKS VODKA

Distillery · Ironworks Distillery
Type · Apple vodka

Ironworks Distillery unites two parts of Nova Scotia heritage—the shipbuilding trade and the apple orchards of Annapolis Valley—in their vodka. Located in a marine blacksmith's shop from 1893, the distillery replaces the coal-fired forges with a German copper still for creating small batch spirits. Apples are ground by hand into a stew of sweet cider and pomace, and fermented with German white wine yeast for up to eight weeks. After 17 hours of double distillation, the final product is blended with water, retaining a gentle taste of the original fruit as well as a hint of butterscotch.

Alc/Vol: 40%
Location: Lunenburg (NS), Canada
Established: 2009

## INDIGENOUS FRESH PRESSED APPLE VODKA

Distillery · Tuthilltown Spirits
Type · Apple vodka

Tuthilltown Spirits revives a tradition of small-batch spirits production in the Hudson Valley that counted more than 1,000 farm distillers before Prohibition: nearly a century later, the 220-year-old Tuthilltown Gristmill was converted into a micro-distillery. Redefining traditions for a contemporary context, their apple vodka begins in the orchards of Tantillos Farm with fresh-pressed apples: the cider is later fermented and distilled in Tuthilltown's twenty-plate copper pot stills. Each bottle contains the spirit of up to 80 apples, with a refreshing hint of fruit and a silky mouth feel.

Alc/Vol: 40%
Location: Gardiner (MT), USA
Established: 2003

## OCEAN ORGANIC VODKA

Distillery · The Ocean Vodka Organic Farm and Distillery
Type · Sugarcane vodka

When you first see the spherical, crystal-blue bottle, you think it must surely contain perfume. You hesitate to remove the cork, for fear of being overwhelmed with an intense burst of the latest industrially produced fragrance. What it really contains, though, is organic vodka from Maui—vodka that is so good Hawaiian Airlines serves it on board its flights. The Smiths, the family behind the spirit, simply use what their magnificent Hawaiian island has to offer: organically grown sugar cane and deep ocean mineral water. The ice-cold water is pumped up from almost 1,000 meters below the Kona coast and then desalinated and filtered. The sugar cane grows in the volcanic soil around the distillery. It is free from pesticides and is harvested by hand.

Alc/Vol: 40%
Location: Maui (HI), USA
Established: 2005

## BLENDED POTATO VODKA

Distillery · Vestal
Type · Potato vodka

The Blended Potato Vodka from Polish distillery Vestal is all about the understatement. But although it is designed to serve as a basis for cocktails and mixed drinks, it certainly has no reason to hide itself away. It is distilled from Innovator, red Asterix, and Russet Burbank potatoes, which are harvested early so that the vodka gets the benefit of their full aroma. In 2010, the year the distillery opened, owner William Borrell, who now lives in London, had to try and sell samples of his vodka by traipsing from one bar to the next. When Waitrose, an upmarket British supermarket, bought 3,500 bottles in one go, he obviously became a very happy entrepreneur. Borrell recommends pairing the Blended Potato Vodka with a dry vermouth and a green olive.

Alc/Vol: 40%
Location: Kartuzy, Poland
Established: 2010

## CORBIN
## SWEET POTATO VODKA

Distillery · Sweet Potato Spirits
Type · Potato vodka

It is not all that long ago that (in Europe at least) sweet potato was considered quite an exotic dish. Nowadays, it has become so commonplace that mushed-up sweet potato is often the first solid food to pass a baby's lips. Little kids just love the creamy consistency and sweet taste—which, as Corbin Vodka shows, stick around even after the tuber has been distilled. David John Souza, the man behind the vodka, is the fourth generation of his family to grow sweet potatoes in California's sun-drenched San Joaquin Valley. In 2007, he expanded the farm by opening the Sweet Potato Spirits distillery, which has been producing the soft, buttery vodka with hints of caramel ever since. The team says that the distinct aroma creates a drinking experience more like a wine than a vodka. The jury at the San Francisco World Spirits Competition were impressed enough to award it double gold.

Alc/Vol: 40%
Location: Atwater (CA), USA
Established: 2007

# Bottled Spuds

•

Potatoes are like humans—some are simply destined for greatness. British farmer William Chase knew for years that his royal potatoes were bursting with untapped potential. But even he was surprised when his Chase Vodka started picking up awards.

It all started with Lady Claire, King Edward, and Lady Rosetta. Those are the illustrious names of the British potatoes that William Chase planted and dug up, year in, year out, on his farm in Herefordshire. Growing potatoes is an arduous task and one that was made all the more thankless by the British climate. Fluctuating harvests and downward price pressure from the supermarkets did not exactly have Chase leaping out of bed in the morning.

When, after a so-so harvest, Chase had to stand back and watch his potatoes go to a potato-chip factory instead of landing in the supermarket vegetable aisles, he decided he had had enough. He also came up with a brilliant idea. Instead of just growing his potatoes, he would also process them himself—into potato chips! That same year, 2001, Chase founded Tyrrells English Crisps

in Herefordshire and started selling Lady Claires, King Edwards, and Lady Rosettas as carefully hand-cooked chips in stylish packaging. His timing was perfect. Bored by industrial products that all tasted the same, chips fans immediately embraced the different flavors and extra crispiness of Chase's snacks. The message behind the chips also chimed with the zeitgeist: consumers, especially those in Europe and the U.S., were becoming fans of handmade regional fare that was produced in a positive way.

The years that followed were exciting times for Chase. He had gone from being a regular British potato farmer to an entrepreneur and global success. He no longer spent his days out in the fields but at his desk, on airplanes, at trade fairs, and visiting his many customers. And yet something was nagging at him. In every harvest, there were still some potatoes that, due to their size or natural deformities, could not be used to make chips. Chase was keen to find some way of using all the undersized, knobbly Lady Claires, King Edwards, and Lady Rosettas. While traveling in the U.S., he came across a potato farm with its own distillery, and his next brilliant idea was born. He would turn the potatoes into vodka.

Once again, the timing was perfect. Secretly a bit bored by all the management work involved in running his new potatochip empire, Chase threw himself into the challenge of setting up his own distillery. He accepted the best of many offers for Tyrrells and became a good deal richer overnight. After doing a lot of research, he bought one of the world's tallest rectifying columns, made a hole in the roof of his barn so that it would fit, and began making vodka. He proudly christened it—the only British vodka to be made entirely from potatoes—Chase Vodka. That was in 2008. Two years later, in 2010, Chase Vodka won the Best Vodka award at the San Francisco World Spirits Competition.

Chase is both proud and disenchanted. It took almost no time at all for his vodka to rank among the best in the world. Critics are full of praise for the soft, buttery spirit made from the potatoes with the illustrious names. He exports his award-winning vodka all over the world. Plus, the message is twice as good this time around: even working with a raw material as apparently unassuming as the homegrown potato, a British farmer can make handcrafted products that completely win over consumers and critics. And he has done it twice in a row.

But something is nagging at him again. It takes 16 metric tons of potatoes to make just 1,000 liters of Chase Vodka. That means he needs at least 135 potatoes to make one bottle. The quality is outstanding, but the margins are less impressive. Although Chase can live with that, he is nevertheless experimenting with British apples from his 200-year-old orchard. Apples are good because they do not have to be planted each year and the yields are higher. Also, domestic cider apples have fallen somewhat into obscurity. Chase now uses them as the basis for Williams Chase Elegant Gin and his Naked Chase Apple Vodka.

# CHASE
# ORIGINAL VODKA

**Distillery · Chase Distillery**
**Type · Potato vodka**

Chase Distillery's Original Vodka is made from King Edward and Lady Claire potatoes. The regal-sounding tubers grow on a Herefordshire farm that is also home to the distillery. William Chase, who spent 20 years growing potatoes, always suspected that they had hidden potential. He first tapped into it with his gourmet potato chips (Tyrrells) and then, shortly after, achieved potato perfection in liquid form. Two years after Chase opened the distillery, his Original Vodka won gold at the San Francisco World Spirits Competition. Produced in the most traditional of ways, the 40% spirit is pure and smooth with a naturally sweet, creamy taste. Superb served neat.

Alc/Vol: 40%
Location: Herefordshire, United Kingdom
Established: 2008

# POMORZE UNFILTERED
# POTATO VODKA

**Distillery · Vestal**
**Type · Potato vodka**

As anyone who has ever made a potato salad will know, overly floury potatoes can ruin the whole endeavor. A potato fact that is not quite so widely known, though, is that different varieties need different climatic conditions and produce very different aromas. William Borrell is well aware of this and applies the knowledge to his Polish vodkas. His Pomorze Unfiltered Vodka is made from red-skinned Asterix potatoes that he grows close to the Baltic Sea. Distilled just once, the vodka retains its full aroma and develops blueberry and licorice notes. Borrell wants to use his vodka to revive the tradition of regional differences in the spirit. He is firmly opposed to multi-distilled, multi-filtered, soulless industrial vodkas. With their authentic flavors, Vestal vodkas have earned themselves a permanent spot in high-class bars such as those at the Ritz.

Alc/Vol: 40%
Location: Kartuzy, Poland
Established: 2010

# Mikkeller Brewery

Once a Beer, Now a Spirit. Many a good beer has been reborn as a good spirit. This is certainly true of Mikkeller's Oloroso Cask Black, a spirit that proves how closely beer brandy and whiskey are related. The basic ingredients of malt, yeast, and water are responsible for the similarities in the taste of the two spirits. Hops can dominate a beer brandy, while whisky has to spend at least three years in wooden casks.

Mikkeller's Copenhagen-based "gypsy brewers" make their beer in host breweries throughout Europe and the United States. The incredibly adventurous craft beers are usually only available in relatively small or even tiny quantities. On top of that, they are often only sold in certain countries or on specific occasions. This allows Mikkeller to wow its global fan base with a staggering number of constantly changing flavors.

Mikkeller also uses host distilleries for its spirits. The Black Series is the heart of the Mikkeller Spirits range and is made using the brand's flagship beer, Mikkeller Black, an imperial stout with an impressive 17.5% alcohol by volume. The beer is distilled in small quantities in the copper still at the multi-award-winning Braunstein distillery in Copenhagen. The process produces a stout brandy, which is then aged for a short time in wooden casks that give the 43% spirit its aroma, flavor, and color. A different sherry, rum, or bourbon cask is selected for each batch. Like the very best whiskeys, the Oloroso Cask Black is aged in sherry-infused European oak casks, whose nutty, chocolaty notes combine perfectly with the spirit's malty flavor.

## MIKKELLER BREWERY BOURBON CASK BLACK

Distillery · Braunstein Distillery
Type · Beer brandy

This spirit is based on one of Mikkeller's most popular beers: Mikkeller Black, an imperial stout that comes in at an impressive 17.5%. The beer is distilled and then put into casks—in this case, casks that were previously used for bourbon whiskey. After being stored for just a short time, the distillate softens and develops the vanilla and caramel notes that are typical of bourbon. For the Mikkeller team, though, it is important that the cask aromas do not get the upper hand. They want the beer distillate to shine through loud and clear so that it appeals to the many beer aficionados who will doubtless be interested in this fine spirit.

Alc/Vol: 43%
Location: Copenhagen, Denmark
Established: 2012

## MIKKELLER BREWERY OLOROSO CASK BLACK

Distillery · Braunstein Distillery
Type · Beer brandy

Back in 2012, Denmark's Mikkeller Spirits began concocting something that was neither whiskey nor bourbon but beer brandy. Its Oloroso Cask Black is made by distilling Mikkeller Brewery's flagship stout. Apparently the biggest challenge was not distilling the beer, but making sure its aroma and flavors did not get lost during the process. The team's collaboration with the Braunstein distillery, also a Danish company, has taught it that the way to overcome the challenge is to do things slowly. The batches are small and exclusive because each one uses a specially selected oloroso cask. This also means that the taste and color vary slightly every time. What Mikkeller can guarantee, however, is that the flavors of nuts, dark chocolate, and dark fruit will make the Oloroso Cask Black a joy for whiskey drinkers everywhere.

Alc/Vol: 43%
Location: Copenhagen, Denmark
Established: 2012

## KIUCHI NO SHIZUKU

Distillery · Kiuchi Brewery
Type · Beer brandy

The Kiuchi Brewery has produced sake and shochu for nearly two centuries, but branched out into beer in 1996 due to changes in Japanese micro-brewing law. Soon after, they built their first distillery and began to experiment with spirits in the form of Kiuchi No Shizuku (in Japanese, "first drip from the distillation kettle"), a unique distillation of the Hitachino Nest White Ale. The witbier is matured in oak barrels with coriander, hops, and orange peel for one month and then distilled again and matured. The pale gold spirit recalls jenever, with notes of malt, citrus, herbs, and woodsmoke.

Alc/Vol: 43%
Location: Kounosu, Japan
Established: 2003

# ALLGÄUER BIERBRAND

Distillery ·
Brennerei-Kelterei Salzgeber
Type · Beer brandy

In 1553, beer brewing was banned in Bavaria during the warm late spring and summer months due to the sour taste of the output. The Märzen beer of early spring would be stored in summer and enjoyed in autumn (later becoming the original beer of Oktoberfest in the nineteenth century). Salzgeber's beer brandy begins with this Bavarian tradition and brings out the soft, malty tones and bitter, hoppy flavors through distillation and several months of aging in lightly toasted chestnut barrels. Allgäuer Bierbrand's hints of vanilla and smoke make it an intriguing alternative for whiskey connoisseurs.

Alc/Vol: 42%
Location: Babenhausen, Germany
Established: 1985

# STICKUM PLUS

Distillery · Stickum Distillerie
Type · Beer brandy

The Uerige brewery and restaurant gets its name from the Düsseldorf regulars who frequented the bar in its early days (it dates back to 1862). They nicknamed its first brewer "der Uerige," or Grumpy. Despite not being the most welcoming of names, it never seems to have put anyone off. In fact, things are going so well that 2007 saw the opening of Destillerie Stickum, which makes beer brandy from two of the brewery's Altbier varieties. Stickum Plus (45%) is distilled from DoppelSticke, a beer designed for the U.S. market. The distilling process reduces 250 liters of beer to 14 liters of spirit that will then age in an oak cask for at least a year. The result is rich in fruit and filled with aromas of honey and malt.

Alc/Vol: 45%
Location: Düsseldorf, Germany
Established: 2007

## NAMIHANA

Distillery · Hawaiian Shochu Company
Type · Shochu

When Ken Hirata first asked shochu master Toshihiro Manzen to train him, Manzen told him he could forget it. Hirata, then 40, had a successful career in finance behind him and was considered too old to undertake the 15-year training. In the end, though, his plan to open a shochu distillery in Hawaii won Manzen over, and Hirata spent three intensive years learning the traditional art of making shochu. When he left for Hawaii, Manzen gave him a 100-year-old fermentation vat that Hirata now uses for fermenting various local varieties of sweet potato (which turns them the most beautiful shade of magenta). His wonderfully smooth, unfiltered Namihana shochu is distilled in a wooden kidaru and aged for six months. Hirata produces just 6,000 or so bottles a year.

Alc/Vol: 30%
Location: Haleiwa (HI), USA
Established: 2013

## OIMATSU
## BENI-IMO

Distillery · Oimatsu Shuzo Co.
Type · Shochu

Oimatsu Shuzo has existed as a sake brewery for more than 200 years and was still in the founding family's hands when the new millennium arrived. 40 years ago, it expanded its repertoire to include shochu, a spirit made from grain, sweet potatoes, or rice. The breakthrough came with its five-year-old, barrel-aged Kojiyadenbei. Tagosaku, a shochu that has a very unusual bouquet thanks to the addition of a white yeast, is very popular in Hita, the town in western Japan that is home to Oimatsu Shuzo. The 25% Beni-Imo shochu is made from red sweet potatoes. It is a connoisseur's drink and features a floral, sweet aroma with notes of roasted chestnuts and mushrooms. Young people in Japan are especially big fans of shochu and these days prefer it to sake. They drink it straight, over ice, or mixed with hot water.

Alc/Vol: 25%
Location: Hita, Japan
Established: 1789

## VINN
## BAIJIU

Distillery · Vinn Distillery
Type · Grain spirit

As anyone who has done business in China will know, declining a baijiu will invariably lead to raised eyebrows from your host. The "white liquor", which is the direct translation of the name, is usually pretty strong stuff and is said to have all manner of magical properties. The Ly family recipe has existed for several generations and has traveled from China to Vietnam and on to Oregon, where it is made today. At their distillery in Portland, the five Ly siblings, who all share Vinn as a middle name, make whiskey, vodka, mijiu, and baijiu. All their spirits are distilled from rice, which means they are all gluten free. Their baijiu is relatively mild (40%) and tastes rather like a white whiskey with hints of sake. It can be enjoyed neat—warmed up if desired—or as a lively addition to a cocktail.

Alc/Vol: 40%
Location: Wilsonville (OR), USA
Established: 2009

## GLENDALOUGH PREMIUM POITÍN

Distillery · Glendalough Distillery
Type · Grain spirit

Glendalough Distillery was set up by five young Irish friends from Wicklow and Dublin (all of whom really suit a beard) as a way of reviving an important part of Ireland's heritage. 2013 saw them launch their poitín, an all-but-forgotten barley spirit that was the forerunner of whiskey and goes back 1,500 years. The first of their three varieties, Premium Poitín, uses an old recipe that calls for the finest sugar beets and malted barley. Their Sherry Cask Poitín is finished in sherry casks, which give it an amber color and deep, woody notes. And at 60% their Mountain Strength Poitín puts an extra kick in cocktails. The distillers prefer their poitín neat over ice, but they also suggest trying it with soda, lemonade, or cola (pot&coke), or even as a rub to treat your aches and pains.

Alc/Vol: 40%
Location: Wicklow, Ireland
Established: 2011

## KOZUBA WHITE DOG

Distillery · Z. Kozuba i Synowie
Type · Rye White Dog

When the three Kozuba brothers decided to make their first whisky crystal clear, it could well have been a deliberate ploy to allay their concerns that the Polish public, so used to vodka, would not touch a darker spirit. What is more, the family-run distillery lies in a very conservative part of the country, a rural area about 150 km north of Warsaw. The trio have been making spirits there since 2005, using ingredients from their largely untouched surroundings. White Dog is distilled in small batches using the finest rye and then aged for just one month in a steel tank. At this point, most other whiskies would take a deep breath before kicking back and relaxing in an oak cask for a few years. Yet despite being what you might call unfinished, White Dog is a consummate spirit, which, with its honey, chocolate, and smoky aromas, is sure to keep even Polish drinkers happy.

Alc/Vol: 40%
Location: Jabłonka, Poland
Established: 2005

## THE WHITE RYE

Distillery ·
Dillon's Small Batch Distillers
Type · Rye White Dog

The Dillons set up their small distillery on the Niagara wine route, in an area that sits directly opposite Toronto on the shores of Lake Ontario. Here they are surrounded by everything they need to make their vodkas, whiskies, fruit spirits, and bitters. Sourcing ingredients locally is of the utmost importance for distiller Geoff Dillon, who taught himself the art of distilling after studying biology and economics. His interest in spirits did not materialize out of thin air: he caught it from his father, a chemist and zoologist with a passion for spirits. These days, Peter Dillon supports his son as an herb and botanicals expert. The White Rye is just one of the prestigious products on offer at Dillon's Small Batch Distillers. To allow the full flavor of the Ontario-grown grain to come to the fore, the Dillons forgo ageing the rye in wood.

Alc/Vol: 40%
Location: Beamsville (ON), Canada
Established: 2012

# STEINREICH

Distillery · Brennerei Sellendorf
Type · Corn schnapps

Korn is the typical fermented grain distillate of Northern Germany, first regulated in the semi-autonomous city of Nordhausen in the 1500s. While Germany could boast of 8,000 agricultural grain distilleries by the end of the nineteenth century, the present-day market is overwhelmingly dominated by mass commercial producers. Steinreich is a unique alternative, lifting this humble spirit through the rigorous distillation of high-quality organic wheat, overseen by master distiller Günter Krause. This high-percentage Korn offers a mild, clean-burning flavor with long-lasting notes of cereal and spice.

Alc/Vol: 42%
Location: Steinreich, Germany
Established: 1780

# EHRINGHAUSEN
# DINKELKORN HOLZFASSGELAGERT

Distillery · Brennerei Ehringhausen
Type · Corn schnapps

Since 1962, the Ehringhausen family has pioneered the sustainable production of organic grain spirits in their ancestral hometown, with a heritage of more than 700 years. Dinkelkorn is their variation on Korn, the traditional North German spirit that is normally based on rye or wheat. Ehringhausen's spirit, made with organic spelt and barley, is distilled in a small copper pot still and matured in bourbon barrels in order to meld and develop the malty flavors; the wood also lends notes of vanilla and dried fruit to the final result. Dinkelkorn is best drunk chilled as an aperitif or digestif.

Alc/Vol: 32%
Location: Werne, Germany
Established: 1962

ABK6 Cognac
75

Pisco
76

Macchu Pisco
82

# Great Grapes

•

Every winegrowing region of the world produces spirits as well as wine. They are made directly from the juice or from the pomace, which is what remains of the grapes after they have been pressed. Many of these fresh or cask-aged brandies are world famous—like cognac, for instance. Others, such as pisco, are still waiting for their global breakthrough.

## BRANDY SOLERA GRAN RESERVA SINGLE CASK ORO

Distillery · Bodegas Rey Fernando
de Castilla
Type · Brandy

As a master distiller, it must be so wonderful to see the first spiderwebs stretched across the oak casks you have just put into storage. The Bodegas Rey Fernando de Castilla gives the eight-legged creatures that inhabit its vaulted cellars all the time in the world to work their silken magic. The distillery, which opened in Jerez de la Frontera in 1837, rests its brandies and sherries for anything up to several decades. The barrels are stacked beneath covered windows that are set high in the walls and keep a cool westerly breeze drifting in and out. The Solera Gran Reserva Single Cask Oro brandy spends 15 years in oloroso casks, which give it a deep mahogany color and a clean, yet complex taste that combines aromas of tobacco, wood, nuts, and figs. It goes particularly well with chocolate or a cigar.

Alc/Vol: 40.6%
Location: Jerez de la Frontera, Spain
Established: 1837

## BIO ATTITUDE COGNAC

Distillery · Léopold Gourmel
Type · Cognac

Pierre Voisin's grandfather must have made a powerful impression on him, seeing as he chose to name his cognac distillery—Léopold Gourmel—after him. What is more, Voisin had to persuade co-founder Olivier Blanc that it was a good idea. The pair set up the business in 1972, but these days Blanc runs it on his own. Despite this change at the top, the name Léopold Gourmel continues to be associated with outstanding cognac. Connoisseurs have been known to fork out 1,000 Euros for a bottle. Blanc has spent the past few years converting his vineyards to organic standards and has received Ecocert certification. His grapes grow in an ideal location in premier cru territory to the south of the town of Cognac. Blanc's Bio Attitude is a new kind of cognac that tastes positively spring-like with its notes of mandarin and fresh walnuts.

Alc/Vol: 42%
Location: Genté, France
Established: 1972

## ABK6 COGNAC

Distillery · Domaines Francis Abecassis
Type · Cognac

ABK6 is one of the three cognac ranges made by Francis Abécassis, a French distiller. He launched it in 2006 to show the younger generation that cognac could also be enjoyed outside of gentlemen's clubs. The unusual name, ABK6, comes from the casual way Francis' daughter Elodie abbreviates her surname in text messages. When it comes to producing the cognac, though, casualness takes a back seat. ABK6 is made with the utmost professionalism. The grapes, all of which come from the official Cognac region, are turned into alcohol using the Charentais distillation process. Cellar master Christian Guerin has an excellent knack for blending the estate's cognacs and can draw on very old stocks in his work. The VSOP Grand Cru (40%) has just been crowned World's Best Cognac by the World Drinks Awards.

Alc/Vol: 40%
Location: Claix, France
Established: 2005

# ABK6 Cognac

Domaines Francis Abécassis is the only French cognac producer to make its brandy exclusively with grapes grown on its own soil. That might sound like a small thing, but it clearly has a big impact. One advantage is that the fruit is grown and harvested entirely under the watchful eye of the company. Another is that it drastically reduces the distances involved. No more than 30 or 40 minutes elapse between picking and pressing the grapes, which prevents unwanted premature oxidation. The characteristic taste of the wine—which is later double-distilled and then aged in Limousin oak casks to produce the cognac—also benefits. Achieved in large part by the sunny location of the Domaine de Chez Maillard in the heart of Charente, the flavor remains more constant with the single-estate approach than it would in a conventional assemblage (made by blending different wines). Experts who know the estate can still pick out the unique taste 10, 20, or 30 years down the line. Age, by the way, is very important in a cognac. The brandy can rest for up to 70 years—and naturally the value goes up as the years go by. Despite this, the people behind Abécassis welcome youthfulness. What is more, while the cognac business is still very much a male-dominated field, Abécassis is run by a woman, who, at 29 years of age, could be considered too young for this job in this industry. Nonetheless, Elodie Abécassis has followed in her father Francis' footsteps and now manages the family business with him. It is very much down to her efforts that ABK6, one of the company's three brands (Le Réviseur and Leyrat are the other two), is particularly popular among young cognac connoisseurs.

# Pisco

•

**Pisco is just now coming out of the shadows to bask in the glow of international appreciation. While both Peru and Chile jostle for the honor of laying claim to this clear brandy, Pisco continues its triumphal march, conquering the hearts of bartenders and barflies alike.**

Life was no bowl of cherries for gold prospectors living in San Francisco during the gold rush of 1848. Very few people actually found any gold, and the town was awash with punch-ups, diseases, fleas, and all manner of other unpleasant things. In the interests of simplicity, anyone looking for a real rush would just reach for the bottle. The most popular drink in San Francisco at the time went by the name of pisco.

Pisco is a spirit made from grape must. It was invented in the sixteenth century in the Viceroyalty of Peru, which was under Spanish colonial rule. The Spanish came to the west coast of South America looking for gold. They arrived with the blessing and in the company of the Catholic Church, in whose rituals wine plays an important role. It was therefore not long before the Spanish started growing grapes in suitable parts of the new colonies. The fruit did especially well in the Isca region of what is now Peru. Soon these vineyards were producing large quantities of wine that, as well as being popular with the church, was also very well

received in the motherland. The wine from the viceroyalty flourished so well and tasted so good that King Philipp II of Spain came to see it as a threat to domestic wine production and banned all imports in the early seventeenth century.

After that, the viceroyalty had to find something to do with all its surplus wine. The most obvious solution was to use it to make brandy. Distillation turned a large quantity of weak alcohol into a smaller quantity of stronger alcohol. The clear brandy was decanted into earthenware containers and shipped out via the port city of Pisco. To keep things simple, the drink soon became known by the same name as the city.

Viticulture and the production of the popular spirit quickly spread throughout the viceroyalty, which covered territory that now belongs to Peru and Chile, among other countries. But politics and geology were not kind to the pisco industry. The disintegration of the viceroyalty triggered a war between Peru and Chile, both of which were seeking independence and more land. Wine-growing came to a standstill in vast areas of the region. Earthquakes and volcanic eruptions laid waste to vineyards and wine cellars, especially those in southern Peru. In the end, though, the resulting bottlenecks in production did nothing to diminish the popularity of pisco.

But how did pisco end up in the gold-prospecting frenzy of nineteenth-century San Francisco? Simple: it was the only spirit available in large quantities at the time. Any town whose population goes from 1,000 to 25,000 within the space of a year needs to get its hands on a lot of supplies very quickly. If the residents are mostly men, adventurers, and from all over the world, then it makes good business sense to stock up on alcohol. In the days before the Panama Canal and the railways, San Francisco, which lies on the west coast of the United States, had to get its goods via the Pacific. Shipping pisco in from Peru and Chile was therefore an obvious solution.

To this day, incidentally, both Chile and Peru claim pisco as their national drink. Over the years, the two countries have passed numerous laws to protect the spirit and regulate its production. Peru claims that pisco is a protected designation of origin, which means that, like champagne, true pisco can only come from Peru. Chile recognizes that pisco originated on territory that now belongs to Peru, but it says that pisco, like vodka, is a generic name, which means it can produce the spirit. The row also extends to the Pisco Sour, with both countries claiming they invented the cocktail.

Despite the vociferous rivalry between Chile and Peru, pisco was, until recently, relatively unknown outside South America. Rudyard Kipling, writing in 1889, might well have said that pisco was compounded of the shavings of cherubs' wings and the glory of a tropical dawn, but it was tequila, mezcal, and cachaça that took up residence in bars the world over while pisco stayed behind as if trapped in a deep slumber. But then craft cocktails and traditional recipes came back into fashion, and many bartenders have spent the past decade bringing old-timer cocktails, such as Pisco Punch, into the present day. It is thanks to their work that pisco is now one of the most interesting contenders for the next spirit to take the world by storm.

## PISCO WAQAR

Distillery · Pisquera Tulahuén
Type · Pisco

One thousand meters above sea level in Tulahuén, Muscat grapevines flourish on the hills above the Atacama Desert, fed by spring water coming down from Andean glaciers. The sweet, fat, rosy grapes have been hand-picked and used to make pisco by five generations of the Camposano family, a tradition now embodied in Pisco Waqar. The master distiller oversees the gradual evaporation of wine in a copper cauldron on a clay oven, preserving the heart of the wine without any distillation, filtering, or wood aroma. The result is a pure, young liquor with the clean, fresh aroma of fruits and flowers.

Alc/Vol: 40%
Location: Tulahuén, Chile
Established: 1850

## PISCO BARSOL

Distillery · Bodega San Isidro
Type · Pisco

Pisco, the Quechua word for bird, gave its name to the Peruvian valley, river, and port, as well as the grape brandy produced in this area for more than 400 years. The historic Bodega San Isidro makes its artisanal Pisco Barsol in a strictly traditional way, distilling Quebranta, Italia, and Torontel grapes in copper pot stills made in the 1800s, without adding water or barrel-aging. Since pisco can only be distilled once, conditions must be perfect—and the bodega incorporates modern technology, including Italian de-stemmers and pneumatic presses, in order to achieve the purest spirit possible.

Alc/Vol: 41.3%
Location: Ica, Peru
Established: 2004

## MACCHU PISCO

Distillery · Macchu Pisco S.A.C.
Type · Pisco

Macchu Pisco is a family-owned company based in Peru and run by Melanie da Trindade-Asher. She has assigned her relatives, including her nearly 100-year-old grandmother, to the parts of the business to which they are best suited. As a graduate of Harvard Business School, da Trindade-Asher can put a lot of that learning to use now, even though certain aspects of the production process for her three piscos are pretty old-fashioned. The grapes, for instance, are crushed with bare feet—and seeing as somewhere between 6 and 15 kilograms of the fruit have to be crushed for every liter of pisco, da Trindade-Asher brings in people from outside the family to help. Her traditional Macchu Pisco is made from non-aromatic quebranta grapes. Only the juice (no pomace) is fermented, distilled, and then left to mature for up to a year. The result is a perfect base for a Pisco Sour.

Alc/Vol: 40%
Location: Ica, Peru
Established: 2003

# Macchu Pisco

Melanie Asher, a young American with Peruvian roots and a Harvard degree, produces pisco with her sister Elizabeth in Ica, Peru. Ever since 2005, when they founded their company, the sisters' award-winning spirits have been a major driver of the pisco boom in the U.S. The story of their company begins when a teenage Melanie was spending time with her family in Peru and tried a few Pisco Sours. She wondered why, when tequila and cachaça were so popular in the U.S., no one knew about pisco. The question stayed with her over the next few years until she wrote her final paper for Harvard Business School. Her study on the successful founding of a pisco distillery won a prize and gave her the motivation she needed. She mustered her courage, asked her family for financial support, convinced her sister to join her when she graduated from Harvard Law School, and set up Macchu Pisco. Melanie is now based in Ica, the main region for pisco production in Peru, and oversees the distillery's three piscos: Macchu Pisco is a classic pisco made of Quebranta grapes; La Diablada is a more flowery number based on a blend of aromatic grapes; and the limited-edition Ñusta is a mosto verde pisco made from partially fermented grapes and presented in exclusive ceramic bottles.

Melanie and Elizabeth share the tasks involved in running Macchu Pisco. Melanie is the master distiller and supervises production in Peru with the help of her 97-year-old grandmother. Elizabeth is the brand ambassador. She travels the world and handles the marketing and export side of the business. The sisters take personal responsibility for every aspect of the company and handle each step on the path that leads from ground to glass. They also campaign for fair working conditions in Peru and for the professional advancement of Latina women in Peru and the U.S. So far, their dedication to high-quality pisco produced under fair conditions has helped their business to grow by thirty percent each year.

## POLI CLEOPATRA MOSCATO ORO

Distillery · Poli Distillerie
Type · Grappa

A still called Crysopea plays a key role in the production of Cleopatra Moscato Oro. Its double boiler vacuum—the only one of its kind in Italy—lowers the boiling point and thereby produces a much more aromatic grappa. Jacopo Poli, who runs the long-standing family distillery, is a crazy kind of guy and makes no bones about it: "When I walk into the stills room, it's second nature for me to stand to attention and then walk along in front of the cauldrons offering a military salute." His respect for the equipment is also the reason why his grappas are so extraordinary. Cleopatra Moscato Oro is made using the fresh pomace of Moscato Fior d'Arancio and Moscato Bianco grapes, which, after spending a short time in oak casks, lend the grappa notes of fruit and honey.

## BOSCO MONTE VECCHIO GRAPPA

Distillery · Catskill Distilling Company
Type · Grappa

The town of Bethel in New York State is best known as the place where Woodstock happened. That could soon all change, though, as the hugely popular whiskey, vodka, and grappa from the Catskill Distilling Company mean that the brand is literally on everyone's lips. While studying to become a veterinarian in Pisa, Monte Sachs, who hails from Connecticut, developed a much greater fascination for distilling grappa. He learned the art from an elderly Italian farmworker and became hooked. In 2009, he and his wife Stacy opened a micro-distillery and saloon in Bethel. His Bosco Monte Vecchio Grappa (42%) is made from Riesling grapes and looks as fresh as the Catskill Mountains spring water it contains. The taste brings to mind roses, pears, and earthy herbs.

## GRAPPA DI GRECO

Distillery · Distilleria F.lli Caffo
Type · Grappa

Giuseppe Caffo was born in 1865 and grew up to become a passionate distiller. His dream of having his own distillery in Santa Venerina on the eastern slopes of Mount Etna finally came true when he turned 50. Caffo then quickly earned himself a reputation as an expert in accurately recreating old recipes. Since then, the baton has been handed from father to son three times and the Gruppo Caffo has grown into a diverse company that runs several distilleries and has a repertoire of 2,000 recipes. One of them is an homage to the Magna Graecia, the parts of Sicily colonized by the Greeks in pre-Christian times. The Greco Bianco grape variety that the settlers introduced is the basis of Caffo's Grappa di Greco, a sweetly aromatic, 42% ode to Greek-Italian friendship.

Alc/Vol: 40%
Location: Schiavon, Italy
Established: 1898

Alc/Vol: 42%
Location: Bethel (NY), USA
Established: 2009

Alc/Vol: 42%
Location: Limbadi, Italy
Established: 1915

### RANSOM
### GEWÜRZTRAMINER GRAPPA

Distillery · Ransom Spirits
Type · Grappa

In 1997, Tad Seestedt invested all of his savings in the hope of realizing his dream of running his own distillery. The product of that investment—Oregon-based Ransom Spirits—began with brandy, eau de vie, and grappa. These were followed in 2007 by whiskey, gin, and vodka. Only Gewürztraminer grapes grown in Oregon are allowed into Seestedt's fruity, intensively flavored grappa. The grapes are pressed very gently to ensure that the pomace retains the typical aromas of the fruit. The pomace is then mixed with water, fermented, pressed, and distilled. Only the "heart of the hearts" gets bottled. The result is a highly aromatic grappa that is extremely smooth on the palate.

### DERRIÈRE LES MURS
### MARC DE CHAMPAGNE XO

Distillery · Champagne Moutard
Type · Marc de Champagne

An empty bottle thrown into the river in Buxeuil would eventually drift through one of the 12 arches of the Pont Neuf in Paris. If you were thinking of sending a message this way, the flacon that Moutard uses for its pomace brandy would be a very eye-catching choice of vessel. In fact, it is so stylish that your message could not be anything other than a handwritten poem. Compared to the Moutard family's 400-year-old winemaking tradition, the distillery in Champagne is really quite young. Around the end of the nineteenth century, Hyacinthe Diligent began developing the spirits that would eventually make the family business famous. Today, cousins Edouard and Alexandre still use his recipes as the basis for products like the intensely aromatic Marc de Champagne XO, which is cask-aged for 10 years.

### VIEUX MARC DE
### CHAMPAGNE

Distillery · Champagne Moutard
Type · Marc de Champagne

The Moutards are old hands when it comes to winemaking. Their names have been appearing in the cellar records of Buxeuil since 1642, which has allowed them to secure themselves a place in that most holy of winemaking regions, Champagne. The clay content of the otherwise very chalky soil allows true connoisseurs to pick a Moutard out of a long line-up. The sunny, southerly location of the Côte des Bar doubtlessly also contributes to the unique aroma. However, those of us who do not possess such finely tuned gustatory senses can still appreciate the quality of the champagne, liqueurs, and chocolates made in this region. The Vieux Marc de Champagne, for instance, is made from Champagne grape must, has been cask-aged for five years, and is the perfect choice for a refined aperitif.

Alc/Vol: 40%
Location:Sheridan (OR), USA
Established: 1997

Alc/Vol: 40%
Location: Buxeuil, France
Established: 1642

Alc/Vol: 40%
Location: Buxeuil, France
Established: 1642

# From Branch to Bottle

•

Capturing the fragrant aromas of fruit, berries, and nuts by maceration or distillation is a long and carefully preserved tradition in many countries. Considered deeply unfashionable and fuddy-duddy for a while, high-quality brandies and liqueurs made from stone fruit, pip fruit, berries, and nuts have now returned to the limelight where they belong.

# Stählemühle

The region around Lake Constance has a long tradition of growing fruit and making fruit brandies. Yet it was a newcomer who, a good ten years ago, brought a breath of fresh air to the industry with his eagerness to experiment, the quality of his products, and even the way he marketed them. Christoph Keller was working as a publisher of art books in Frankfurt am Main when he began to long for a more peaceful life, rural surroundings, and an agricultural challenge. His quest to fulfil those desires brought him to Lake Constance, where he purchased a mill called Stählemühle. The building came with an old *Abfindungsbrennrecht,* which meant whoever owned the mill could distill alcohol at a better tax rate than usual. Not wanting to let the perk go to waste, Keller learned the fine art of distilling schnapps and, within a very short space of time, began causing quite a sensation. His limited-edition brandies made of wild fruit, old orchard fruit, and single varieties of herbs were soon in high demand and are now often sold out before they have even been bottled. These days, Keller is considered one of the world's greatest schnapps distillers. His spirits are sold in the finest hotels in Germany and beyond. Yet despite its success, the entire business is still run by one inquisitive, careful distiller and his wife, Christine. A few neighbors also pitch in. Their help is especially welcome when Stählemühle is producing Monkey 47 Schwarzwald Dry Gin, for which Keller, as the master distiller, is responsible. Keller and his business partner, Alexander Stein, developed the gin together and brought it to the world's attention. It is safe to say that the Lake Constance region, where craft and creativity have always played an important role, is now one talented artisan richer than it was before.

## NR. 239 SICILIAN BLOOD ORANGE "MORO"

Distillery · Stählemühle
Type · Fruit brandy

For a blood orange to fully develop its delicately bitter bouquet, it needs regular variations in temperature, heavy frosts at night, and a consistently dry climate. This fine fruit brandy from Stählemühle uses only Sicilian blood oranges that are grown right on the slopes of Mount Etna. Locals describe the pleasantly bitter aroma of the fruit as moro. The oranges have to be processed gently, so Christoph Keller uses warm maceration followed by a precisely calibrated distillation. This produces a wonderfully dense, highly aromatic blood orange brandy.

## HIEBL WALDBROMBEER-BRAND 2013

Distillery · Destillerie Hiebl
Type · Fruit brandy

To ensure that his fine brandies achieve a perfect harmony of color, aroma, and taste, Georg Hiebl pays special attention to treating nature's gifts with care. His family-run company has been producing brandies and liqueurs of the highest quality since 1997. Since numerous varieties of fruit grow in the region where he lives—Austria's Mostviertel—he sources most of his raw materials from the local area. The wild blackberries he uses for this brandy have a particularly intensive taste and lend the spirit a robust, ripe blackberry aroma. The brandy exerts a powerful pull. It is intensely fragrant on the nose, and fresh and pleasantly spicy on the palate.

## VOGELBEERBRAND

Distillery · Capovilla Distillati
Type · Fruit brandy

Over the years, Vittorio Capovilla's formerly ink-black, bushy eyebrows have turned an elegant white. Nevertheless, he can still climb the trees on his four-hectare orchard close to Bassano del Grappa as energetically as he could in the mid-eighties when he began his second career as a fruit distiller. Capovilla uses rare, difficult-to-process fruits like wild plums, wild cherries, and sloe berries to produce around 50 crystal-clear brandies. "It's all fruit that you won't find in any supermarket," says Capovilla, who does not mind the low yields in the slightest. Take his rowanberry brandy, for instance: about three percent of the hand-picked harvest ends up producing the spirit, a 41% brandy with an herbaceous flavor and characteristic bitter-almond tones.

---

Alc/Vol: 42%
Location: Eigeltingen, Germany
Established: 2004

Alc/Vol: 40%
Location: Haag, Austria
Established: 1997

Alc/Vol: 41%
Location: Rosà, Italy
Established: 1986

# Capovilla Distillati

There are two ways of meeting the Capo, or boss: either you try the spirits that bear his name, or you go and meet the man himself. Vittorio "Gianni" Capovilla, a.k.a. the Capo, is a Venetian master distiller who puts an exceptional amount of passion into making his high-proof products. This means you are very likely to find him up a ladder, tasting the fruit hanging heavy on the trees in his orchard. The Capo manages four hectares of what is, essentially, a real-life Garden of Eden. He began distilling back in 1974, when his bushy eyebrows had yet to turn the gray they are today. The fruits of his childhood came first—elderberries, wild plums, Cornelian cherries—but he soon added other varieties to the brandies he was producing. "I'm lucky to have found friends who are happy to pick wild pears and sloe berries with me on the weekends," says the Capo with a smile. But picking the organically grown fruit by hand is not enough. The distillery, which lies just shy of an hour's drive northeast of Vicenza, also places the utmost importance on the proper techniques for chopping and distilling the various type of fruit. Machines built by the Capo himself ensure that these standards are met. When the spirits are ready, the machines take a back seat again as the bottles are labeled and sealed by hand on the premises. Incidentally, the Capo does not confine his activities to his native Italy. A more recent passion for distilling rum led him and his friend Luca Gargano to begin doing just that on the Caribbean island of Marie-Galante. The microclimate there yields an especially rich sugar cane, the legendary canne rouge B47.259, which is the basis of Rhum Rhum, a double-distilled rum aged in used French wine barrels.

## KOHLER
## HEUMÄDER QUITTE

Distillery · Destillerie Kohler
Type · Fruit brandy

Before a quince embarks on the long journey to the bottle, it gets a special kind of treatment. Stuttgart-based distillers Eberhard Kohler and Lars Erdmann know what will push quinces to the outer limits of flavor development: "frosty nights." When the fully ripe fruit is harvested from around the distillery and the Swabian Alps in the fall, the velvety down that covers them has to be rubbed off by hand to get rid of its bitter taste. The quinces are then cut up (no easy task), ground, and pressed for juice. After that, they go into the mash—minus the must and pomace—and are left to ferment slowly at low temperatures. Once finished, the brandy has transformed the scent of raw quinces into something you can actually taste: a marmaladey mix of honey, citrus fruits, pears, and apples.

## FAUDE FEINE BRÄNDE
## ZIBÄRTLE

Distillery · Hausbrennerei Kaiserstuhl
Type · Fruit brandy

Florian Faude is barely 30 years old, but he has already been running his own distillery for almost a decade. His interest in agriculture stems from his winemaking education, resulting in hand cultivation in the steep hills of the upper Black Forest. Zibärtle is one of their most renowned products, due to the painstakingly laborious process of harvesting the native species of wild zibarte plums. The small fruits are shaken from their trees and picked clean, and the greenish-yellow flesh is separated from the stones. The distillation process results in a rare flavor, reminiscent of almonds.

## BRENNEREI ZIEGLER
## VOGELBEERBRAND

Distillery · Edelobstbrennerei
Gebr. J. & M. Ziegler
Type · Fruit brandy

Ziegler has maintained a 150-year commitment to high-quality spirits based on a deep understanding of origin, soil, and climate. Using only fully ripe, undamaged fruit from renowned wine-growing regions in Europe, the distillery manages the fermentation and brandy production with clockwork precision and a cultivated nose for separating the heart of the distillate. Their idiosyncratic Vogelbeerbrand, with its rich marzipan notes, is made with rowan fruit retrieved from the wild by expert pickers who can distinguish it from the nearly identical but bitter-tasting fruit of mountain ash trees.

Alc/Vol: 40%
Location: Stuttgart, Germany
Established: 1953

Alc/Vol: 40%
Location: Bötzingen, Germany
Established: 2006

Alc/Vol: 48%
Location: Freudenberg am Main, Germany
Established: 1865

# HAFERPFLAUMENBRAND

Distillery · Weingut Danner
Sort · Fruit brandy

The Danner winery practices the principles of Slow Food as well as traditional family knowledge, passed down since 1715, in the Ortenau region of the Black Forest, where a rare strain of damson called the "oat-plum" is cultivated attentively. Three times per harvesting season, only the fully ripe fruit is collected to make a particular kind of schnapps. In the cellar, the spirit is distilled in wooden barrels, which not only enable precise temperature control but also reinforce the notion of "terroir"— the wood itself is cut from the surrounding forest and aged for three years before use.

Alc/Vol: 42%
Location: Durbach, Germany
Established: 2006

# WILDE EIERBIRNE

Distillery · Manufaktur Jörg Geiger
Type · Fruit brandy

As a VIP in the village of Schlat in the Swabian Jura, it is standard practice to pose for photos while holding a piece of fruit. It is, after all, impossible to avoid the fruit-growing aspect of the local economy (the other big sector is sheep rearing). The wild pear in Jörg Geiger's hand does not look small because of his size but because these pears never get big, even when they are fully ripe. These *Eierbirne*, which are invariably bursting with flavor, grow on trees that are often more than 100 years old. Geiger gets the pears from farms within 60 kilometers of his distillery. To preserve the aroma of the fruit, the pears are cold-fermented and the first distillation happens before the end of the fermentation process. After resting, a second distillation produces the finished product. In the end, one liter of pure distillate contains up to 30 kilograms of the wild pears.

Alc/Vol: 42%
Location: Schlat, Germany
Established: 1995

# APFEL IM KASTANIENFASS

Distillery · Manufaktur Jörg Geiger
Type · Fruit brandy

Distillery owner and boss Jörg Geiger is lucky that he was born in the area. For one thing, it means he speaks the dialect of the Swabian Jura, and for another, it means he understands the mentality. If that were not the case, all his attempts to collaborate with the local farmers would probably have been doomed to failure. As it is, however, he has persuaded the some 300 farmers and estate owners in the region to allow him to turn the fruits of their meadow orchards into premium liqueurs, brandies, and sparkling wines. A happy side effect is that it ensures the ancient varieties keep growing and that it puts a few fair euros away in the bank. What the brandies lack in numbers, they more than make up for in flavor. Apfel im Kastanienfass is a 42% barrel-aged apple brandy.

Alc/Vol: 42%
Location: Schlat, Germany
Established: 1995

## REISETBAUER
## KAROTTE

Distillery · Reisetbauer Qualitätsbrand

Type · Fruit brandy

Hans Reisetbauer is renowned for the purity of his brandies, the result of his devotion to his orchards and the mix of precision and inventiveness in his distillation process. No detail goes unexamined: even the choice of water has been considered, now coming exclusively from the springs of the Mühlviertel. Karotte is one of his most famous spirits: each bottle contains the distillate of 23 kilograms of locally-grown carrots. The vegetables are fermented, mashed, and twice-distilled in a copper alembic still, designed by Reisetbauer himself and fabricated by Christian Carl of Göppingen.

Alc/Vol: 41.5 %

Location: Axberg, Austria

Established: 1994

## TESLA
## ŠLJIVIO

Distillery · Tesla Distillers

Type · Fruit brandy

Boris Marki did not like the fact that none of the really good cocktail bars in Frankfurt stocked any Croatian spirits. He knew they were worthy of a place on those shelves, so he began combing Croatia for a distillery that could help him develop a slivovitz that would be a real asset to cocktails and long drinks. The result was Tesla Šljivovica, made from a blend of Croatian plum varieties distilled separately. Enjoying it neat and unchilled brings its fruity, plummy aromas to the fore, while adding Sprite, a few ice cubes, and some lemon turns it into the ideal drink for sipping at the bar on a night out. But what does all this have to do with Nikola Tesla, the man who inspired the name? Well, he was a Croatian by birth and a strong opponent of prohibition. Also, he had a really great moustache that is nice to look at.

Alc/Vol: 42 %

Location: Zagreb, Croatia

Established: 2013

## NAHMIAS ET FILS
## MAHIA

Distillery · Baron Nahmias

Type · Fruit brandy

A long time ago, when Jews were in the majority in Morocco, they started making alcohol from fruits that grew in the Mediterranean region. They called the result mahia. As is the case with spirits in many other cultures, the name means "water of life". A few years back, a new distillery brought mahia production to the U.S. The couple behind the venture base their version on figs, but their Moroccan heritage means they know that dates and grapes are also traditional mahia ingredients. At the end of the distilling process, the mahia is flavoured with anise, probably one of the most quintessential aromas of the Mediterranean.

Alc/Vol: 40 %

Location: Yonkers (NY), USA

Established: 2012

# Nahmias et Fils

David Nahmias grew up in Taznakht, a small town in the Atlas Mountains of southern Morocco. When he was a young boy, he would often stand with his mother in their kitchen and watch alcohol bubbling away. They had collected figs, chopped them up, and allowed them to ferment for several days before putting them into the family's still to turn the mash into mahia, a centuries-old brandy made by Moroccan Jews.

Mahia, which, just like eau de vie, means water of life, combines the sharpness of grappa with the oriental flavors of fig and aniseed.

"I remember the smell of the fermenting figs and the alcohol," says Nahmias, recalling the many times he helped his mother at the still. When he got older, Nahmias went to school in Paris and later studied in Montreal before going to New York. The smell of the mahia distilling remained with him as a constant reminder of his childhood, his home, and his family, but as time went on, the memory became more and more distant.

When the financial crisis struck the U.S. in 2009 and his parents, the last link to his old life, died, Nahmias decided to make some changes. He left his job as a software developer and, together with his wife Dorit, who had just lost her banking job, set about reviving his family's tradition by turning it into a business.

Their small distillery in Yonkers, just a few kilometers north of the Bronx, produces a kosher mahia that has won numerous awards. Although it has made a few concessions to Western taste buds and the times, it still tastes and smells very much like it did back in Taznakht.

The company is a dream come true for Nahmias. More than just giving mahia its rightful place on drinks menus across the U.S., it has allowed him to continue his family's generations-old tradition. His respect for that tradition is reflected in the distillery's name, which points to the future as well as the past: "We hope our children will continue what we have started," says Dorit. "They are eager to learn and are very proud of their heritage."

## ROCHELT
## WACHAUER MARILLE

Distillery · Tiroler Schnapsbrennerei
Rochelt
Type · Fruit brandy

Günter Rochelt was 49 before he made a career out of distilling his own spirits—a passion the Austrian had held since the 1970s. He started out making spirits in his cousin's garage from fruit that grew in the family's orchards, and eventually founded Schnapsbrennerei Rochelt in 1989. A few years later, in 1993, the German edition of *Playboy* magazine ran an article on the distillery, entitled A Sensual Drug. Günter's son-in-law now makes 21 types of fruit schnapps, among them this apricot brandy. The spirits are naturally fermented and twice-distilled according to an old Tyrolean tradition. They are unfiltered and only use the finest, ripest fruit. Compromises are a no-go: "If conditions are less than ideal, we will not harvest that particular year," say the Rochelt Principles, which are set in stone—and available to read on the website.

Alc/Vol: 50%
Location: Fritzens, Österreich
Established: 1989

## KIRSCHWASSER

Distillery · Hausbrennerei Baumgartner
Type · Fruit brandy

Hausbrennerei Baumgartner lies close to the border with France and Switzerland. In 1983, Fridolin and Anneliese Baumgartner decided to add to their vineyard business (the fruits of which they sell to a local cooperative) by making their own spirits. They turned a barn into a distillery and got to work. Their first product was pomace brandy, which is still one of Fridolin's favorite types of schnapps. His wife, however, prefers the 43% kirschwasser. Along with their Mirabelle brandy, it recently won gold and the title of brandy of the year at the Destillata international spirits competition. The cherries, which the couple grow themselves, have an unbeatable Brix rating. Even distilled to a crystal-clear brandy, the fruit retains its intense aroma and delivers nuances of vanilla, cinnamon, and dark chocolate.

Alc/Vol: 43%
Location: Vogtsburg-Oberbergen, Germany
Established: 1983

## MARDER EDELBRÄNDE
## MIRABELLENBRAND

Distillery · Brennerei Marder
Edelbrände
Type · Fruit brandy

In 1950s post-war Germany, large helpings of good food became a bit of an obsession. This also led to a rapid increase in the amount of alcohol people were consuming. Just as West Germany was about experience its economic miracle, Otto Marder founded his distillery close to the Swiss border. The location meant that he could easily get his hands on surplus fruit for his still. The company, which is now run by Otto's grandson, Stefan Marder, has over 40 brandies and liqueurs on offer. They are made in the traditional way, using berries, wild fruit, and stone fruit that the distillery purchases and then processes. The Mirabelle plums that lend their name to this particular brandy come from either the Black Forest or the region around Nancy, depending on the year. The spirit is bursting with intense aromas of the fruit, incorporates flavors from the stone, and "is also popular with women," says Stefan.

Alc/Vol: 40%
Location: Albbruck-Unteralpfen, Germany
Established: 1953

## CLEAR CREEK
## WILLIAMS PEAR BRANDY

Distillery · Clear Creek Distillery
Type · Eau de Vie

Three decades ago, Oregon farmer Stephen McCarthy decided to use the fruits of his abundant harvests for another purpose—he preserved them as brandy or eau de vie. He learned his craft from distillers in the region between France, Switzerland, and Germany, whose William pears resemble the Bartletts grown at Mount Hood for over a century. The pears are crushed and fermented whole using Champagne yeast, and the mash is then distilled and aged for several months. The colorless, clear liquid offers a strong pear nose with a clean aftertaste, a rare example of a fruit brandy with American origins.

## EAU DE VIE
## DE SUREAU NOIR

Distillery · Distillerie Gilbert Holl
Type · Eau de Vie

Gilbert Holl began his craft as a home distiller in Alsace, transforming the plums, raspberries, and cherries of his harvest into traditional eaux de vie. Since achieving official authorization in 1984, his distillery has grown to produce tens of thousands of liters of pure alcohol with an expanding palate of ingredients, from wild elderberries and dandelion flowers to more esoteric strains like cumin, ginger, kiwi, and even sauerkraut. Still produced in small batches of 150 liters, the artisanal methods of maceration and distillation preserve a rigorous tradition of high-quality brandies.

## LAURENT CAZOTTES
## GOUTTE DE PRUNELART

Distillery · Distillerie Artisanale
Laurent Cazottes
Type · Eau de Vie

The prunelart grape was nearly eradicated in the late nineteenth century by phylloxera, the sap-sucking bane of European vines that lacked resistance to the American insect. In the 1990s, the species was resuscitated from a few conservatory specimens, but the deep violet grape is still a rarity, grown on only two hectares in France. Cultivating a quarter of that area through biodynamic practices, distiller Laurent Cazottes creates his brandy attentively: the grapes are left to dry on the vine, then picked by hand, stemmed and seeded, crushed, fermented, and distilled into an exceptional eau de vie.

Alc/Vol: 40%
Location: Portland (OR), USA
Established: 1985

Alc/Vol: 45%
Location: Ribeauvillé, France
Established: 1978

Alc/Vol: 45%
Location: Villeneuve sur Vère, France
Established: 1998

# The Somerset Cider Brandy Company

Burrow Hill lies in southern Somerset, a county in the southwest of the U.K. It is a very pretty, very hilly, very English place. The weather is mild, the fields are green, and there are apple orchards everywhere you look. This is the home of the Somerset Cider Brandy Company.

Cider has been made in the area around Martock for more than 150 years. Cider brandy, an English version of Normandy's Calvados that dates back to 1678, returned about 25 years ago. When Tim Stoddart and Julian Temperley, the men behind the Somerset Cider Brandy Company, set about reviving the tradition in the late 1980s, they had to invest a lot of passion and energy in tackling the stubbornness of the authorities, the Calvados associations, and the conservative British market.

"At the start of my cider career, I would often be asked why I didn't just make Calvados. My answer was always: I don't want to go to jail. We never did get to make Calvados, so we came up with a friendly cousin instead," says Temperley. In the end, the Somerset, Cider Brandy Company was granted the first cider distilling license in recorded English history.

The soil conditions—known as the terroir, like in viticulture—on the 65-hectare farm are ideal for cider-making. The orchards produce over 40 varieties of apple that go by such fabulous names as Brown Snout, Stoke Red, Harry Masters, and Kingston.

Every fall, a carefully balanced mix of sour, sweet, and bitter apples is fermented to produce a must with an alcohol content of five percent, which is then stored over the winter. The must is then double distilled in two 180-year-old copper stills (Josephine and Fifi) between March and April, before going into oak casks to age for anything up to 20 years.

"I think that our Somerset Cider Brandy products have given many people a completely new view of, and pride in, Somerset's cider traditions," says Temperley. What is more, the EU granted Somerset Cider Brandy official status as a protected geographical indication in 2010.

## SOMERSET
## CIDER BRANDY (5 YEARS)

Distillery · Somerset Cider Brandy Co.
Type · Cider Brandy

The cider brandy made in Somerset is not only an achievement of craft but also of legal status. The process of distilling cider was first banned by William of Orange in 1678, and the recent revival championed by Julian Temperley was threatened when EU directives excluded the distinctive British spirit from a protected definition of brandy as a grape-based spirit. In 2011, Temperley finally won recognition for the brandy made from apples grown in Burrow Hill. The cider is fermented and distilled in spring and then matured in oak barrels for five years to develop a velvety palate and spicy aftertaste.

Alc/Vol: 42%
Location: Somerset, United Kingdom
Established: 1987

## CALVADOS PRESTIGE

Distillery · Pierre Huet
Type · Calvados

François Huet, began the Huet family Calvados tradition so quietly that almost no one noticed. He used his bumper apple crops to make the spirit and stored it in bottles on his estate in Cambremer, Normandy. François' son, Pierre—from whom the cellar gets its name—did an excellent job of bringing it to the public. Paul Bocuse and Michel Guérard, both famous chefs, hold Huet Calvados in especially high regard. Today, the family-run estate continues to grow more than 25 varieties of apple in four levels of acidity. Early apples, harvested in September and October, are the best for making Calvados. The spirit is aged in oak casks for a minimum of two to three years. Depending on how old it is, the color of the Calvados can be anything from pale gold to a deep amber—though it takes half a century for it to reach that end of the spectrum.

Alc/Vol: 40%
Location: Cambremer, France
Established: 1865

## BOURBON BARREL AGED APPLE LIQUEUR

Distillery · Warwick Valley Winery & Distillery

Type · Fruit liqueurs

Warwick Valley Winery spent about a decade experimenting and succeeding with wines and ciders before it added a distillery in 2002. It was the first to open in the Hudson Valley since prohibition. Inspired by traditional French and German recipes, the American Fruits range features brandies and liqueurs made using fruit sourced from the fertile region around the Hudson River. The Bourbon Barrel Aged Apple Liqueur is a sweet cider blended with the winery's own apple brandy and aged in bourbon barrels. The result is a one-of-a-kind 19.5% dessert wine that combines smooth apple notes with a smoky caramel finish.

Alc/Vol: 19.5%
Location: Warwick (NY), USA
Established: 2002

## PÜR LIKÖR WILLIAMS

Distillery · Brennerei-Kelterei Salzgeber

Type · Fruit liqueurs

Kiki Braverman bridges the gap between the Old World of traditional German distilling and the New World of California. Her pür·spirits begin in her native Bavaria with fresh, organically grown ingredients, from sloe, juniper, and raspberries to the legendary elderflowers from the forests around Lake Constance. Under the leadership of master distiller Franz Xaver Salzgeber, the spirits are distilled in small batches of several hundred bottles. This liqueur is made with pears that are harvested and then stored to develop their aroma. At peak ripeness, they are crushed and put into bottles. Imagine over six kilograms of pears in one bottle!

Alc/Vol: 25%
Location: Babenhausen, Germany
Established: 2007

## GOLDEN MOON DRY CURAÇAO

Distillery · Golden Moon Distillery

Type · Fruit liqueurs

Although it was founded in 2008, Colorado's Golden Moon Distillery is traced with historical elements and references. The four stills date from the early 1900s, the artisan production processes are faithful to the techniques of the mid-1800s, and the research library preserves rare books on distillation dating as far back as the 1500s. The Dry Curacao combines the peel of the small bitter oranges from the eponymous Caribbean island, while saffron, cinnamon bark, and rooibos add a mellow spice, gaining depth and a rich, natural golden color through light aging in oak barrels.

Alc/Vol: 40%
Location: Golden (CO), USA
Established: 2008

# AMARETTO-LIQUEUR

Distillery · Destillerie Dwersteg
Type · Nut liqueurs

Destillerie Dwersteg has evolved for over a century under a family of distillers; recognized for their uncompromising quality, they maintain a commitment to organic ingredients and production. The distillery even runs on renewable energy, including wind, hydroelectric, and solar. At the same time, they pursue fair trade practices in sourcing their ingredients, like bourbon vanilla from Madagascar or raw cane sugar from the Philippines and Paraguay. Combining the sweetness of caramel with bitter almonds, their Amaretto-Liqueur is a distinctive counterpart to champagne or lemon juice and ice.

Alc/Vol: 20%
Location: Steinfurt, Germany
Established: 1882

# LANTENHAMMER WALNUSSLIQUEUR

Distillery · Destillerie Lantenhammer
Type · Nut liqueurs

When late summer rolls around, the fruit growing in Upper Bavaria feels almost duty-bound to reach the pinnacle of its ripeness—partly because doing so will complete the beautiful scenery at the foot of the Alps and partly because it will raise its chances of being picked to star in a fruit brandy. Destillerie Lantenhammer in Hausham, close to the shores of Schliersee, uses only the most sun-drenched fruit from carefully selected regions for its brandies, fruit cuvées, and liqueurs. Its walnut liqueur, however, is based on an old recipe that makes it the exception to the distillery's rule. To achieve the desired full-bodied notes, the liqueur uses nuts that are still green and therefore not fully ripe. The flavor is enhanced with bourbon vanilla, and the liqueur can be enjoyed neat, with coffee, or as part of a cocktail.

Alc/Vol: 30%
Location: Hausham, Germany
Established: 1928

# Monasteries

•

**Many monasteries began running their artisan distilleries and cellars long before the much younger craft scene started to get interested. Chartreuse proves that a big brand can still do things the monastic way.**

"Hip" is not necessarily the first word that springs to mind when someone mentions monasteries. Yet many of them have spent centuries operating the kind of small-scale distilleries and wineries that are now proving so popular in the much younger craft scene. Distilling on a large scale can also still be done the monastic way, as the Chartreuse brand proves. Warnings issued to monks and priests about drinking too much alcohol are roughly as old as western monastic culture itself. Guidelines on how to be a good monk, therefore, do not just deal with prayer and the issue of receiving gifts but also address the consumption of wine. Writing in his Regula in the sixth century, Benedict of Nursia, the founder of western monasticism, said that monks should have no more than a hemina (probably about a quarter of a liter) of wine per day: "Although we read that wine is not at all proper for monks, yet, because monks in our times cannot be persuaded of this, let us agree to this, at least, that we do not drink to satiety." If a monastery had less wine than that, or indeed none at all, Benedict urged those monks to "live without murmuring."

All respect for its effects aside, wine was mainly intended to be a risk-free thirst quencher. "Wine was the safe option in the Middle Ages. Water was often contaminated and, because of the risk of cholera, could kill you. Wine, by contrast, was sterile," says Martin Erdmann, an expert on monastery products at Manufactum, a German retailer that sells durable products manufactured in traditional ways. Its Gutes aus Klöstern range specializes in monastery-crafted goods and has everything from moisturizers and mustard to beers, wines, and spirits.

"The wine didn't usually taste very nice, so people would add herbs to it. Vermouth, for instance, was invented that way," says Erdmann. The monks also drank beer, which is still a popular monastery product today, especially in Belgium and the Netherlands. Brewing was a way of preserving grains. Stronger drinks, such as schnapps and liqueurs, have their roots in herbal medicine. "Curing illnesses is in the bible, after all," says Erdmann, who once served as a novice monk. "If you got sick in a monastery, you had a much greater chance of recovering." Aside from a few palaces, it was

the monasteries that gathered knowledge about treating illnesses, since working with Greek, Latin, and Arabic documents was common practice for them. Monks preserved ancient learning about the medicinal effects of herbs.

The monasteries often came across recipes by chance, but they had the expertise necessary to decode and follow them. Extracting active substances from herbs required strong alcohol. "Whiskey is actually the oldest monastery spirit of them all," says Erdmann. It is thought that whiskey was being distilled in connection with St. Patrick—in Scotland and Ireland—as early as the fifth century. Evidence for whiskey distilling only starts in the fifteenth century, though. "The strange thing is, no matter where you look in the world today, you will not find a single monastery with a whiskey distillery," says Erdmann. That aside, an enormous variety of monastery liqueurs and schnapps is available today. The most famous of all is probably Chartreuse (which even

made it into East German pop history when it was referenced in the 1963 hit *Kartäuser Knickebein Shake).*

In 1605, François-Annibal d'Estrées, a Marshal of France, presented the recipe for "an elixir of long life," which contained 130 herbs, to Carthusian monks at Vauvert, near Paris. Today, the Chartreuse distillery has the largest liqueur cellar in the world. It guards the recipe for its elixir like the precious treasure it is. Only two monks know the secret formula. When they travel, they travel separately so that if anything happens to one of them, the information will not be lost. Wooden cases made by the monks for transporting the liqueur are proof that they had begun trading Chartreuse by the eighteenth century.

The liqueur was originally intended to be taken as a medicine in very small doses with sugar or in tea. These days, the high alcohol content (69%) means that the label can no longer mention the beneficial effects of the drink.

Since 1857 the friars of the Maristenkloster in Furth, Lower Bavaria, have been producing herb brandies and liqueurs according to traditional recipes with ingredients from the cloister garden.

In monasteries that still run distilleries, the spirits and liqueurs are usually produced by hand and in small quantities—as is the case at the orthodox Dreifaltigkeitskloster in Buchhagen, Germany, which is home to just four monks. "When you visit an orthodox monastery, you are immediately served a schnapps, a cup of strong coffee, and a glass of water," explains Erdmann, who is a big fan of the Buchhagen monks' wild cherry liqueur. "They do the steeping in preserving jars. It's a wonderful drink, but they only make a couple of bottles a year." Italy also has a large number of similarly minimalist distilleries. Their products can sometimes be quite unusual, such as the eucalyptus liqueur made by the Tre Fontane monastery near Rome, and the rhubarb-root liqueur from the secluded Monastero di Camaldoli near Arezzo.

So far, none of the monasteries have dared to try opening a whiskey distillery. Erdmann thinks any that did could look forward to a golden future: "With the right technique and the right casks, they'd do a roaring trade!"

## ZWETSCHGENWASSER

Distillery · Klosterkellerei Erzabtei
Sankt Ottilien

Type · Fruit schnapps

The Erzabtei St. Ottilien, a monastery that lies some 40 kilometer west of Munich, is home to around 100 Missionary Benedictines. The monks aim to be as self-sufficient as possible when it comes to feeding themselves and their guests—and with crops, cattle, pigs, and chickens, they do very well at achieving their goal. They also process any surplus herbs and fruit from the monastery nursery and orchards to stop them going off. The 40% Klosterlikör, which is made using a secret blend of herbs, won the audience award at the Destille Berlin Festival in 2014. As for the fruit brandies—apple and pear, plum, and Williams pear—the monks handle the entire production process themselves, from growing the fruit to labeling the bottles. And just in case anyone was about to jump to the wrong conclusions: the spirits are, of course, never used for missionary purposes.

Alc/Vol: 40%
Location: Sankt Ottilien, Germany
Established: 1884

## AVADIS
## HASELNUSSGEIST

Distillery · Avadis Distillery
Type · Fruit schnapps

The Vallendar family has been distilling fruit brandies for several generations. The estate in Wincheringen-Bilzingen, which lies a few kilometers from Germany's border with Luxembourg, dates back to 1824. While their father had other commitments (agriculture and viticulture) that meant he could only ever pursue his beloved distilling as a hobby, brothers Andreas and Carlos Vallendar have dedicated themselves to professional distilling. Visitors to the Avadis distillery and spirothek can assess the duo's talents for themselves by trying the whiskies, liqueurs, and brandies on offer. Avadis' 40% hazelnut brandy, for instance, is a delicious mix of intense caramel and nougat flavors that leave you with a sense of having just enjoyed a spoonful or two of chocolate-hazelnut spread.

Alc/Vol: 40%
Location: Wincheringen, Germany
Established: 1824

## HIMBEERGEIST

Distillery · Alfred Schladerer Alte
Schwarzwälder Hausbrennerei

Type · Fruit schnapps

The Alfred Schladerer distillery has been manufacturing fruit brandies since 1844, now in the sixth generation of the Schladerer family. Their Himbeergeist begins with wild raspberries, hand-harvested in the Carpathian Mountains between the Republic of Moldova and Ukraine, and transported to Staufen within two days. There, the brandy is produced using Black Forest spring water, without added sugar or additives, highlighting the sweet flavor of the berries granted by the rich climate and soil in which they are grown. Finally, the brandy is bottled in Schladerer's signature four-sided bottle.

Alc/Vol: 42%
Location: Staufen im Breisgau, Germany
Established: 1844

## KOHLER INGWERDESTILLAT

Distillery · Destillerie Kohler

Type · Herb brandy

Ginger schnapps is especially popular among women and has long been considered a women's drink. This casts both the drinkers and the drink in a very fine light indeed. The version produced by grandfather-grandson duo Eberhard Kohler and Lars Erdmann at Destillerie Kohler in Stuttgart delivers its soft, warm, intense flavor with a subtle bite. Making the crystal-clear schnapps involves a complex six-month process, followed by three months of ageing, and then gentle filtration. The combination of essential oils and lime (with no additives) is warming in winter and refreshing in summer.

## EVERSBUSCH DOPPELWACHHOLDER

Distillery · Brennerei Eversbusch

Type · Herb brandy

This juniper spirit is based on a 200-year-old recipe brought from the Netherlands back to Germany by Peter Christoph Eversbusch, a soldier in the Napoleonic Wars and the great-great-great-grandfather of the Eversbusch distillery's current owners. The process has changed little, using the same fine rye distillate and Tuscan juniper berries for several generations, and even the same copper alembic built in 1817. Today, the distillery itself is witness to the events of the twentieth century, from the introduction of refrigeration in neighborhood houses to the transformations of the Second World War.

## ART IN THE AGE ROOT

Distillery · Greenbar Craft Distillery

Type · Herb brandy

In the 1700s, Native Americans taught Pennsylvania settlers their folk recipe for root tea, brewed with wild herbs and roots. The drink would later be adapted for the Prohibition era as alcohol-free root beer. Root returns to the natural potency of root tea as a full-bodied spirit, reflecting the blend of historical tradition and innovative distillation practiced by Art in the Age Craft Spirits. Honoring the sustainable ethos of golden-age American libations, Root boasts a rustic, smoky flavor with aromatic notes of birch, vanilla, citrus, and peppery spices, with entirely organic ingredients.

Alc/Vol: 40%
Location: Stuttgart, Germany
Established: 1953

Alc/Vol: 46%
Location: Hagen, Germany
Established: 1780

Alc/Vol: 40%
Location: Philadelphia (PA), USA
Established: 2008

Nine Leaves Distillery
124

Tres Hombres
128

Kōloa Rum Company
132

Avuá Cachaça
135

# Caribbean Delights

•

Rum and the Caribbean have been inseparable ever since
Columbus introduced sugar cane to the islands. While eighteenth-century European aristocrats were sweetening their
tea with sugar, people in the Caribbean were distilling rum
with what was left after sugar production. Sailors transported it and pirates seized it. Sugar plantation owners grew
rich, while Africans, captured and forced to work as slaves,
lost their freedom and very often their lives. All of them, to a
man, drank rum.

# BUSTED BARREL
# SILVER RUM

Distillery · Jersey Artisan Distilling
Type · Silver Rum

Krista Haley and Brant Braue work really well together in the distillery, but that is where it ends: "We'd kill each other if we had to go home together," laughs Haley. She met Braue when she was looking for something that would balance out her day job as an attorney. He shared her willingness to take risks, her passion for rum, and her absence of fear at the thought of opening a distillery. They bottled their first batch of Busted Barrel Silver Rum, distilled from Louisiana molasses, in August 2013. Two months later, they began bottling their Dark Rum, which is aged in white oak casks, features hints of vanilla and caramel, and brings to mind fine American whiskeys. Both rums have won silver medals from the New York Wine & Spirits Competition. Spurred on by those successes, Haley and Braue are now planning to make flavored rums as well as gins and even whiskeys.

Alc/Vol: 40%
Location: Fairfield (CT), USA
Established: 2013

# CRUSOE
# ORGANIC SILVER RUM

Distillery · Greenbar Craft Distillery
Type · Silver Rum

While many craft rums offer a sweet complexity to classic cocktails, the indulgence can hardly be called altruistic. Greenbar's silver rum, however, can be enjoyed without any guilty aftertaste: by using lightweight bottles with recycled labels and planting one tree in Central American rainforests for every bottle sold, the distillery has developed a certified carbon-negative product. After fermenting molasses and white wine yeast, Greenbar follow with micro-oxygenation, a technique used by California winemakers. The result is a white rum with a dense sugary aroma and a grassy, caramel finish.

Alc/Vol: 40%
Location: Los Angeles (CA), USA
Established: 2004

# OWNEY'S
# RUM

Distillery · The Noble Experiment NYC
Type · Silver Rum

The Noble Experiment's rum is a study in simple, high-quality ingredients: the sugar cane molasses is not completely refined, retaining a unique flavour reminiscent of cane juice, batch-grown in independent plantations in Florida and Louisiana, and matched with a particular strain of yeast. The final factor is New York water, famed for its role in the city's bagels and pizzas and now responsible for this full-flavored white rum, balancing sweet and tropical notes with earthy, smoky undertones. Named after rum-runner "Owney" Madden, the drink seeks to bring native rum back to the United States.

Alc/Vol: 40%
Location: Brooklyn (NY), USA
Established: 2012

# CHALONG BAY
# RUM

Distillery · Andaman Distillers
Type · Silver Rum

Rum was invented in the Caribbean in the seventeenth century using sugarcane, a plant that Christopher Columbus brought to the West Indies in 1493. But in Southeast Asia, the crop has been cultivated for millennia, a history that Chalong Bay now honors through the distillation of rum on the eastern coast of the island of Phuket. Made with a traditional French copper still, this artisanal rum is set apart by its fresh aroma with notes of citrus, coconut milk, flowery honey, vanilla, and licorice. Avoiding industrial methods, Chalong Bay's dedication to sugarcane reinvents a heritage at its origin.

Alc/Vol: 40%
Location: Phuket, Thailand
Established: 2012

124

# Nine Leaves Distillery

For Yoshihari Takeuchi, the road to rum—and fame—involved a mixture of car parts, craftsmanship, and twists of fate. In 2013, he became the owner of Nine Leaves, the first rum distillery on Japan's main island. It is also probably the distillery with the fewest employees, as Takeuchi-san is the owner, distiller, bottler, and driver all in one. Whenever he is not working at Nine Leaves, he is at the family-run company that grew out of his grandfather's woodworking business and now makes automobile parts. Takeuchi-san says that, up until a few years ago, he knew nothing about distillation or rum. But he comes from a family that takes pride in monozukuri—a Japanese term for craftsmanship. He wanted to do more than just produce parts for clutches. He dreamed of making his own product, something that used only Japanese ingredients. As soon as he decided on rum, he set about sourcing the best water, the best sugar cane, and the best craftsmanship he could find.

Takeuchi-san found the perfect source of spring water at a deserted mine close to Lake Biwa in Kyoto Prefecture. The water there is very soft and extremely clean. It took a year for him to get approval for building his small distillery there. That gave him enough time to travel to the Okinawa Islands in the south of Japan and find the best sugar, made directly from boiled sugar cane juice. Unlike other rum producers, Takeuchi-san eschews molasses and sugar cane juice; dark muscovado sugar is the open secret of his rum. He uses Japanese yeast to start the fermentation process. The distillation equipment is the only part of the set-up to come from outside Japan. It hails from Forsyths, a Scottish manufacturer recommended to him by Ichiro Akuto, founder of the Chichibu whisky distillery, which is where Takeuchi-san learned the art of distillation in just three days.

Takeuchi-san currently offers three different rums. Nine Leaves Clear, a double-distilled white rum, won silver in the Innovation de l'Année category at Rhum Fest Paris in 2014. Nine Leaves Angel's Half is a golden rum that comes in two varieties: one that is aged for six months in French oak casks and one that spends six months in American oak casks. The distillery is also currently ageing a brown rum in wine casks from California's Napa Valley. Like whisky, it will spend more than three years in there, so fans of Nine Leaves will have to do as Takeuchi-san says and be patient.

## NINE LEAVES
## ANGEL'S HALF

Distillery · Nine Leaves Distillery
Type · Gold Rum

Yoshihari Takeuchi is a car-parts supplier for Toyota who one day decided he would rather produce rum than gears. He now runs a distillery just outside Kyoto. The sugar cane, which comes from Okinawa, undergoes two rounds of distillation, a technique that he learned while satisfying his thirst for knowledge at Chichibu whisky distillery. Takeuchi says that he is a bit pedantic and analyses the alcohol every five minutes to make sure the flavors are just right. He takes personal responsibility for bottling and numbering his liquid treasures, and (if time allows) delivers the rum to nearby retailers himself.

Alc/Vol: 50%
Location: Shiga Prefecture, Japan
Established: 2013

## MIKKELLER BREWERY
## RUM CASK BLACK

Distillery · Braunstein Distillery
Type · Gold Rum

Denmark's Mikkeller Brewery is still making its far-out beers, but it has also expanded its operations to set up Mikkeller Spirits, which collaborates with external distilleries. For its Rum Cask Black (43%), Mikkeller partnered up with the Braunstein distillery and embarked on a near-blasphemous venture: distilling beer (its 17.5% Mikkeller Black stout, to be precise). Distilled in small batches, the beer makes its way from the copper still into rum casks from the Caribbean island of St. Croix. The result is a beer brandy that combines the fruitiness and hoppy flavor of the beer with a sweet silkiness derived from the rum treatment. And if you are still skeptical about distilled beer, think about this: Rum Cask Black took double gold at the San Francisco World Spirits Competition.

Alc/Vol: 43%
Location: Copenhagen, Denmark
Established: 2012

### TRES HOMBRES
### RUM XVIII 2014

Distillery · Aldea/Oliver & Oliver
Type · Gold Rum

The name Tres Hombres refers to three merry adventurers from the Netherlands and Austria who dreamed of finding a sustainable approach to transatlantic transport. They eventually took the plunge and bought an old fishing boat, in which they now regularly set sail. The Tres Hombres are all about fair trade and conserving resources—principles that are very much in evidence with this rum from the Dominican Republic. Veteran master distillers from Cuba apply their expertise to blending the rum, which is a mixture of older and younger sugar-cane distillates produced using the solera process commonly associated with sherry. The alcohol is then spirited across the ocean to Europe using nothing but the power of the wind. No emissions, no compromises.

### SIMON'S KÖNIGLICH-
### BAYRISCHER-MARINE RUM

Distillery · Feinbrennerei Simon's
Type · Gold Rum

The portrait on the bottle's label commemorates the man who laid the foundations for the Simon's distillery. In 1879, Johann Simon acquired a permit to start distilling spirits at his estate in Spessart, Bavaria. Today, his great-great-grandson Severin is carrying on the tradition and continues to heat the stills with firewood from the estate's own forest. That aside, he also dared to take a step into brand-new territory and fulfil his dream of producing a German rum. Since sugar does not grow in Europe, he opted for a solution that would surely have made Johann proud: a sailing ship brings the Caribbean sugarcane molasses across the Atlantic to Europe. The ingredients might have travelled a long way, but they have plenty of time to start feeling at home while the rum ages in its Spessart oak casks.

### KŌLOA
### KAUA'I SPICE RUM

Distillery · Kōloa Rum Company
Type · Gold Rum

When the Kōloa Rum Company began operating on the island of Kaua'i in 2008, it picked up on a tradition of rum-making that goes back some 200 years. Its Kaua'i Spice Rum is golden and rich with the scent of spice cake, caramel, and vanilla. Ask exactly what spices go into it, though, and you will not get very far. The distillery keeps the details of the blend very close to its chest. One of the key ingredients, though, is water. When rain falls on Wai'ale'ale mountain, which rises 1,500 meters above sea level, it filters down through volcanic strata and into underground aquifers. The Kōloa team says the water has the perfect mouthfeel and, combined with the island's sugar cane, makes a truly unique and delicious rum.

---

Alc/Vol: 40.7%
Location: La Palma & Dominican Republic
Established: 2010

Alc/Vol: 40%
Location: Alzenau, Germany
Established: 1879

Alc/Vol: 44%
Location: Kaua'i (HI), USA
Established: 2008

# Tres Hombres

Whenever the Tres Hombres is moored in a Caribbean port and casks of rum are being loaded into her great wooden belly, crowds of people gather on the quayside to watch, longing etched on their faces. The beautiful old schooner brings cargo from the Caribbean to Europe and back, stopping off at islands in the Atlantic and turning heads in every port she visits. The Tres Hombres is an ambassador for a new, carbon-neutral approach to shipping. She spirits her cargo across the ocean with no engines, no emissions, and only the wind propelling her forward. Very often, she will have a precious cargo of rum onboard.

The three men behind the venture (hence the name Tres Hombres) met, unsurprisingly, out at sea. During a transatlantic crossing, Arjen van der Veen and Jorne Langelaan from the Netherlands and Andreas Lackner from Austria had the idea of transporting cargo with a sailing ship as an environmentally friendly alternative to the gigantic container ships that are used today. It took a fair while for them to realize their dream. In 2008, they bought a 60-year-old fishing ship that had been used in the war and, with the help of many enthusiastic supporters, invested countless hours in turning it into an engineless two-masted ship.

Like a legal version of the smuggling ships of days gone by, Tres Hombres has been transporting very special editions of rum to Europe since 2010. The crew and the ship spend up to two months at sea, braving the elements in order to bring their precious cargo safely into the home port of The Hague. Once there, the first modern-day rum to travel green is bottled and sold throughout Europe under the same name as the ship. The Tres Hombres has so far made four trips to supply its growing fanbase with rum made by renowned blenders and distillers from the Dominican Republic and the Canary Islands. Fourteen casks equate to about 4,500 bottles of Tres Hombres Rum—and once they are all sold out, you just have to wait for the Tres Hombres to return. Alternatively, you could book one of the trainee sailor spots and become part of the adventure.

## KŌ HANA
## HAWAIIAN AGRICOLE RUM

Distillery · Manulele Distillery /
Kō Hana Distillery
Type · Rhum Agricole

What makes agricole rum special is that it is produced using freshly pressed sugar cane juice rather than molasses. Robert Dawson, founder of the Kō Hana Distillery in Hawaii, spent many years learning about cultivating sugar cane. A lot of the island's old varieties had fallen victim to hybrids, so he set about reviving them and planted them around his distillery. They are harder to grow and can only be harvested by hand, but that is a price Dawson is willing to pay for the unique flavors that make each variety different to the next. The cane is harvested when it is at its most flavorsome. The single-variety juice is pressed within 48 hours, fermented with cocoa yeast, and then distilled once. The white rum goes straight into stylish bottles, while the dark rum spends a while in oak casks so it can develop its distinctive color.

Alc/Vol: 40 %
Location: Kunia (HI), USA
Established: 2011

## ST. GEORGE CALIFORNIA
## AGRICOLE RUM

Distillery · St. George Spirits
Type · Rhum Agricole

In 1982, Jörg Rupf founded St. George Spirits in a decommissioned naval hangar, a characteristic move for the German pioneer of the American craft spirits revival. The distillery's California Agricole Rum is unique in its exclusive use of California-grown sugarcane. The stalks are milled by hand to extract fresh juice, which is fermented and distilled in small batches in a copper still, resulting in a rum with truly vegetal aromatics evoking wet grass and truffles. They also make a reserve, which is aged for four years in French oak barrels, tempering the grassy flavor and imbuing spice notes.

Alc/Vol: 43%
Location: Alameda (CA), USA
Established: 1982

## RHUM VIEUX AGRICOLE
## BRUT DE FÛT 2003

Distillery · La Distillerie Bielle
Type · Rhum Agricole

Columbus must have felt a bit like a god when he sailed around the Lesser Antilles in 1493, naming them as he went. The name of his ship provided the inspiration for Marie-Galante, a small, almost spherical island to the south of Guadeloupe. Just 150 years after Columbus discovered it, the first French settlers began growing sugar cane on the island. Since the eighteenth century, it has been producing more white and dark rums than anything else. Back then, the Bielle family were running a coffee plantation, but later switched over to making sugar and then rum. The business is no longer in the family's hands, but it still distills rum the traditional way. Its unfiltered 2003 Brut de Fût, made from freshly pressed sugar cane juice, is aged for eight years, bottled at cask strength, and toys with sweet, bitter, and peppery notes.

Alc/Vol: 53.4%
Location: Grand-Bourg, Guadeloupe
Established: 1910

## MEERMAID INFUSED RUM

Distillery · Meermaid Infused Rum
Type · Flavoured Rum

The idea to create his own spiced rum came to Stefan Walz when he was co-owner of Berlin's Tabou Tiki Room, a bar focused on rum from around the world. Despite the diversity of the stock, Walz wanted to make a flavored rum at a reasonable price and a quality far superior to the industry standard. Meermaid Infused Rum is made with Trinidadian and Jamaican pot still rum, infused for two weeks with 17 natural ingredients, including fresh fruit, dried fruit peel, and spices. By adding and removing these ingredients one by one, Walz has perfected a recipe for a unique, handcrafted infused spirit.

Alc/Vol: 40%
Location: Berlin, Germany
Established: 2013

# Kōloa Rum Company

Kauaʻi, which also goes by the name of the Garden Isle, is not the best-known island in Hawaii, but it is the oldest. No one is sure when exactly Polynesian settlers brought sugar cane to the island and planted it there. What we do know, however, is that the Hawaiian Islands began cultivating the sweet crop long before Captain James Cook came across the Pacific archipelago by chance in 1778. Once Hawaii had been "officially" discovered by the Western world, it did not take long for missionaries, adventurers, and entrepreneurs to begin making their way to the islands in pursuit of new business opportunities. Very quickly, growing sugar cane became one of the biggest industries on fertile Kauaʻi. Plantation workers soon learned how to turn molasses, the sticky byproduct of sugar production, into a high-proof spirit that went by the name of rum.

The Kōloa Rum Company was founded in 2008 as the island's first and only distillery. Despite the general downturn in the sugar cane business, it wanted to try and retain a small part of the long-standing industry by using local sugar cane to produce a sustainable, premium product. The rum is distilled in small batches using a copper still that was made by Liberty Coppersmiths in Philadelphia, Pennsylvania, in 1947. Once it was up and running, the company did not have to wait long to taste success. Its twice-distilled rum made from crystalized raw cane sugar and pure water from Mount Waiʻaleʻale, which has one of the highest rainfalls in the world, received numerous awards just a few years after the first batch was bottled. The Kōloa Rum Company makes unaged white, gold, and dark rum, as well as a coconut rum that is a flavorsome homage to Hawaii and its nature.

## KŌLOA
## KAUA'I DARK RUM

Distillery · Kōloa Rum Company
Type · Dark Rum

The Hawaiian island of Kaua'i is home to just one licensed rum distillery. The Kōloa Rum Company, which sits just outside the town of Kalaheo, is all about capturing the tastes and smells of its balmy surroundings. Its Kaua'i Dark Rum combines hues of coffee and molasses with notes of brown sugar, vanilla, roasted nuts, cotton candy, and burnt orange peel. The recipe is so good that the rum has taken gold four times at the Miami Rum Renaissance Festival. All Kōloa rums are twice distilled in a fully refurbished copper pot still that was made by Liberty Coppersmiths of Philadelphia in 1947.

## ROGGEN'S RUM

Distillery · Tuthilltown Spirits
Type · Dark Rum

Tuthilltown Spirits partnered with the Huguenot Historical Society of New Paltz to produce their Roggen's Rum, a limited-edition aged rum that evokes the history of Hudson Valley trade and cultivation. The Roggen brothers were Swiss immigrants that spread the trade of rum to communities along the Hudson River. Their namesake is made of thick, sweet Louisiana blackstrap molasses, which is diluted, fermented, twice-distilled, and aged in oak casks previously used for whiskeys. The resulting dark rum, free of any added flavour or coloring, has been compared to cognac in its depth and richness.

## AVUÁ CACHAÇA
## AVUÁ PRATA CACHAÇA

Distillery · Fazenda da Quinta
Type · Cachaça

Fazenda da Quinta, a family-run distillery in rural Brazil, is entirely dedicated to the country's national drink, cachaça. Far from the hustle and bustle of Rio de Janeiro, the producers take their time turning their hand-harvested sugar cane into a mash. Natural yeast cultures from the local area produce the base wine, which is then distilled in a copper still. After that, the Avuá Prata cachaça gets six months to recover from the exertions of the distillation process. More haste, less speed, basically. The calm approach to production matches the popular image of Brazil as a country full of sun, beaches, and palm trees—all enjoyed with a wonderfully refreshing cachaça, of course.

---

Alc/Vol: 40%
Location: Kaua'i (HI), USA
Established: 2008

Alc/Vol: 46%
Location: Los Angeles (CA), USA
Established: 2003

Alc/Vol: 42%
Location: Carmo, Brazil
Established: 2013

# Avuá Cachaça

Marco and Roberto are responsible for ploughing the sugarcane fields at Fazenda da Quinta. The oxen are part of Katia Espírito Santo's strategy for producing cachaça in a sustainable, natural way. Santo, the owner of this long-standing sugarcane plantation and distillery in Carmo, Brazil, is one of the country's few female distillers and a great believer in doing things by hand. Following in the tradition of her grandfather, Francisco Alves, who bought the fazenda in 1923, Santo sees to it that the sugarcane is harvested and bundled by hand, and then pressed in a water-powered mill.

The dried solids that remain after pressing—known as bagasse—are either fed to the oxen or used to heat the copper still in the distillery. The freshly pressed sugarcane juice immediately begins to bubble and ferment. Wild yeast ensures that enough alcohol (approx. 15 to 18%) is produced within 24 hours to allow distillation to begin.

Santo's cachaça is made exclusively from her own sugarcane crops. Like a good wine, the cachaça from Fazenda da Quinta has a terroir and each vintage is different to the next. Sunshine and rainfall also have a big effect on the subtleties of the sugarcane's flavor and therefore on the taste of the artisan spirit. Simply by smelling and tasting a cachaça, experts can tell what type of sugarcane was used to make it and what kind of soil the cane grew on.

In addition to her own brand, Santo also bottles (by hand, of course) Avuá cachaça for export. Avuá is the brainchild of the three friends Pete Nevenglosky, Nathan Whitehouse, and Mark Christou. Unwilling to put up with the fact that it was impossible to buy a good artisan cachaça in their native United States, the trio began importing it themselves. They offer two varieties: the mildly herbaceous Avuá Prata Cachaça, which is rested in stainless steel casks for several months before bottling; and the fuller-flavored Avuá Amburana Cachaça, which is aged for two years in casks made of Latin American amburana wood.

135

# Mexico's Favorite Exports

•

Almost 100 years after the Mexican revolution helped tequila go from being a much-derided spirit for the poor to a patriotic national drink, its long-forgotten big brother, mezcal, is being rediscovered. Hopefully it will be able to avoid the excessive industrialization that was tequila's fate.

# Mezcal

•

**The word mezcal comes from one of Mexico's native languages and means "baked agave" Unlike its close relative tequila, mezcal remained largely untouched by industrial production methods until just a few years ago. To this day, most mezcal relies on fairly tough manual labor and is made in small or very small quantities.**

Over just a handful of years, mezcal and its complex, smoky, earthy aromas have won a sizeable place in the hearts of bartenders and spirits aficionados alike. The seemingly overnight success of this Mexican agave brandy has inspired numerous reports depicting its traditional production methods: men in hats harvesting the agaves with machetes and axes, smoky fire pits, mills driven by donkeys, bubbling fermentation vats, and clay stills in palm-roofed huts. With modern consumers collectively longing for authentic products, mezcal has suddenly made child's play of outdoing the all-powerful tequila, that most industrialized of spirits, and becoming everyone's new favorite Mexican export. Given its sudden rise to fame, even those who know the scene inside out are unclear about a few things: what can mezcal actually do, and where has it been all this time?

The Mexican state of Oaxaca, which is named after its capital city, is considered the heartland of mezcal production. It is home to a particularly wide variety of agave plants, or magueys, as they are known in Mexico. The country has 200 native species, and over 30 of them are used for making mezcal. The rarer varieties are usually collected in the wild, while others (such as espadín) have been cultivated for generations. Below the pine-covered mountain slopes, on the rocky soils found in sunny valleys and on hot plains, the plants flourish naturally or are planted in endless rows by human hand. Agave has been part of the Central American landscape for countless millennia, and the history of people in Mexico is closely tied up with it. Early Mexicans used the thorny plants and their long, fleshy leaves to make clothes, tools, building materials, food, and alcoholic drinks.

It is not entirely clear whether distilled mezcal was being produced in Mexico before the Spanish conquest, although some archeological evidence of agave cooking does imply that this was the case. Alternatively, the magueys might simply have been fermented to produce a kind of wine. What we do know, however, is

that the Spanish brought more advanced distillation techniques (with which they had been familiar ever since the Arab conquest of Spain) to Central and South America. They also introduced their habit of marking all manner of occasions by drinking large quantities of high-strength aguardiente. This proved instrumental in increasing the production and distribution of mezcal.

However, distillation using stills and water cooling appears to be the only technological advance that mezcal production has made since the arrival of the Spanish. Like few other spirits in the world, mezcal is closely interwoven with its terroir and the traditions and rites of the people who make it. The *maestros mezcaleros*, the master mezcal distillers, pass their centuries-old

knowledge down through the generations and are often thought of as local celebrities.

Traditionally, the *maestros mezcaleros* oversee the production of handcrafted mezcal from start to finish. The quality of the distillate depends heavily on something that comes at the very start of the process: harvesting the agaves at the right time. From the time the seed is sown, it takes at least six to eight years for an agave to be ready for harvest. At that stage, the plant is just about to reach sexual maturity and its core (or heart) has amassed the maximum amount of carbohydrates. Unripe agaves produce weak mezcal. Harvesting the plants is real backbreaking work. Super-sharp machetes and axes are used to hack away the hard outer leaves. This reveals the heart, which weighs about 50 to 80 kilograms and, thanks to its pineapple-like appearance, is known as the *piña*. The piña is dug out of the ground and then taken with the rest of the harvest to the *palenque,* or local distillery. Depending on the available technology, the piñas travel by donkey, ox-drawn cart, or pickup truck.

Once they arrive, the piñas are baked—although the process is actually more of a cross between steaming and smoking. Thick logs from native trees are burned to charcoal in a deep pit and covered with big stones. The piñas are then piled on top of the hot stones and covered with agave fibers, palm leaves, and soil. They stay in the hot oven for at least three days. During that time, the polysaccharides in the agave hearts are converted into fermentation-friendly sugar. The smoke also has a major impact on the flavor of the finished spirit. When the magueys have swapped their original white for a caramel-brown color, the baking process is over.

Once the magueys have cooled, they are chopped up and ground into a liquid mush either by hand or using a horse-drawn millstone. For the fermentation, the juice, flesh, and water are put into large vats made of either wood or leather. Wild yeast and bacteria (nothing else) cause the mixture to start bubbling and fermenting. When the bubbling stops, the sour, bitter liquid and the solids it contains are distilled for the first time—either in handmade clay vessels or copper stills. The *maestros mezcaleros* decide how many times it has to be distilled to produce the required strength (45 to 55%) and the desired aroma. A simple piece of technology allows them to continually check the quality of the mezcal: they suck up a bit of the liquid using a tube, and then let it splash out into a flat earthenware container. This produces small, pearl-like bubbles, whose structure and consistency give the masters clues about the strength and quality of the mezcal. An experienced *maestro mezcalero* only has to smell and taste a mezcal to know

everything about how it was produced: the types of agave used, whether or not the plants were harvested at the right time, what baking method was used, how long it was fermented for, and how many times it was distilled.

Even though mezcal aged in wooden casks is available to buy (reposado and añejo), many connoisseurs are of the opinion that freshly bottled mezcal provides the most authentic taste and that, unlike with whisky or rum, the woody notes from the cask only harm the complexity of the intense flavors achieved by handcrafted mezcal. The spirit's earthy, smoky notes are inspiring mixologists all over the world to come up with new and exciting cocktails—but if you really want to experience the spirit of mezcal, then there is only one way to drink it: neat.

## TOBALÁ MEZCAL

Distillery · Del Maguey
Type · Mezcal Joven

The Mexican region of Oaxaca produces the most diverse mezcals imaginable. Each one differs according to the variety of the agave used, where it grew, and at what altitude. The Del Maguey brand works with family-run mezcal distilleries in villages throughout the region, pays fair wages, and obtains every type of mezcal flavor it is humanly possible to achieve. One of the specialties is made from tobala agave, a wild variety that is like a truffle in that it grows in the shade of oak trees, but unlike a truffle in that the trees are in high-altitude canyons. It is smaller than the more common espadin, so eight times as many agave hearts are needed to make a mezcal. Water is the only other ingredient in this near-alchemical recipe that takes a spiky plant and coaxes from it the juiciest mango and warmest cinnamon notes.

Alc/Vol: 45%
Location: Oaxaca, Mexico
Established: 1995

## REPOSADO CON GUSANO

Distillery · Wahaka Mezcal
Type · Mezcal Reposado

Wahaka Mezcal is a collaboration between mezcal aficionados from Mexico City and Alberto Morales, whose family has been producing mezcal for five generations. Dedicated to organic farming and sustainable, community-oriented business practices, Wahaka revives centuries-old traditions in order to create a truly modern artisanal spirit. Using farmed agave as well as wild strains from the Oaxacan lowlands and mountain peaks, they offer a range of different mezcals: from the Reposado with the traditional gusano (agave worm) to updated vegan pechugas that use local herbs or apples for distillation.

Alc/Vol: 40%
Location: San Dionisio Ocotepec, Mexico
Established: 2010

## MEZCAL LOS DANZANTES REPOSADO

Distillery · Destilería Los Danzantes
Type · Mezcal Reposado

In 1997, a group of restaurateurs known as Los Danzantes opened a mezcal distillery in Santiago Matatlán, Oaxaca. Their aim was to produce an authentic, handcrafted mezcal that they could serve in their restaurants. Waiting is part and parcel of the complex production process. Things can only get started when the agaves are in bloom and that takes ten years. Once harvested, the agave is roasted below ground in huge pits and then crushed using a millstone powered by Sanson the horse. After that, a long period of natural fermentation begins. "We play banda music to keep the people and the yeast in a good mood," say the Los Danzantes. Music is one of the key ingredients in the mezcal, which is available as Espadín Joven and Tobalá Joven, and as the barrel aged varieties Reposado and Añejo. The guys also make a few rewarding experiments with wild agave varieties, herbs, and creole chicken.

Alc/Vol: 43%
Location: Santiago Matatlán, Mexico
Established: 1997

## LOS AMANTES
## MEZCAL REPOSADO

Distillery · Los Amantes
Type · Mezcal Reposado

Los Amantes refers to the ancient Aztec legend of Mayahuel, the goddess associated with maguey, otherwise known as agave. Their mezcal, produced by families and small distilleries in Oaxaca, begins with the piña (heart) of eight-year-old tobala and espadín agave plants: it is extracted, smoked in conical pits for three days, crushed and fermented, and double- or triple-distilled in copper pots. The Reposado and Añejo varieties are also barrel-aged for six months and three years, respectively. The mezcal balances the delicate smokiness from the cooking process with bright citrus flavors.

## FIDENCIO MEZCAL
## PECHUGA

Distillery ·
Fabrica de Mezcal del Amigo
Type · Mezcal Joven Pechuga

Fidencio Mezcal's Pechuga is the Jimenez family's synthesis of cultural traditions from the Santiago Matatlán region and the seasonal fluctuations of the plant harvests. The Pechuga begins with agave harvested in the new moon, ax-split and roasted in a stone-lined earthen pit, and crushed with a rose quartz stone drawn by the horse Rocio. The fermented agave is then distilled three times with macerated fruit; the traditional chicken breast, said to soften and round out the mezcal, is suspended in the bell of the still. The Pechuga is full-bodied, with ripe notes of fruit and a slight hint of game.

## REAL MINERO
## PECHUGA

Distillery · Real Minero Mezcal
Type · Mezcal Joven Pechuga

The word "production" does not go nearly far enough to describe the ceremony-like approach that the Ángeles family takes to making its mezcals. It all begins with Don Lorenzo, the head of the family, harvesting wild varieties of espadín, largo, barril, tobalá, arroqueño, and tobaciche agave. Following a recipe that is now in its fourth generation, the Ángeles then roast, ferment, and distill the agave hearts. A wooden cross appears regularly throughout, to seal every step with a blessing. To make sure the blessings have the desired effect, Don Lorenzo follows up the roasting (which lasts several days and happens in an earth-covered pit) with some diligent, filling, pre-distillation work: he conducts a taste-test of every single piña. Once those that pass muster have been distilled in clay containers, Doña Florentina fills and labels the mezcal bottles by hand.

---

Alc/Vol: 40%
Location: Tlacolula de Matamoros, Mexico
Established: 2002

Alc/Vol: 47.3%
Location: Santiago Matatlán, Mexico
Established: 1888

Alc/Vol: 50%
Location: Santa Catarina Minas, Mexico
Established: 1889

# Mezcal Sanzekan

Mexico's mezcal distillers have been passing down the secrets of their craft from one generation to the next for centuries. Mezcal is used to appease the gods, honor the dead, bless marriages, and celebrate harvests. Every region has its own rites and traditions that are almost always based on one of the local agave varieties. In the Chilapan region, which lies in the state of Guerrero, the agave in question is cupreata, known locally as maguey papalote. This variety, which has thick, roughly egg-shaped leaves, grows on rocky slopes at 1,500 to 2,000 meters above sea level. Mezcal's increasing global popularity means that (despite the isolation of this mountainous region) pressure has been growing on farmers and maestros mezcaleros to harvest the slow-growing plants and sell them to industrial mezcal producers. While this certainly brings money in the short term, it also means that there will eventually be no more papalote for the local people to sell and enjoy.

In order to strengthen their position, the residents of Chilapan have formed a cooperative called Sanzekan Tinemi, which means "forwards together" in Aztec. The 20 maestros mezcaleros in the cooperative put their faces to Sanzekan mezcal and stand up for the message behind Sanzekan Tinemi: "Neither maguey nor mezcal has any meaning without our people and our culture. This is why we always ensure that the profits from our products find their way back into the communities that preserve our traditions."

# Mezcaloteca

The Mezcaloteca in Oaxaca's old town is a place of pilgrimage for mezcal fans keen to learn about its history and artisanal production. Inquisitive travelers and spirits connoisseurs come to the non-profit cultural association for tastings and workshops that will teach them more about the true spirit of mezcal. The staff are absolutely committed to sharing their respect for mezcal, for its role in Mexican culture, and for the maestros mezcaleros who make the spirit for their local community in the traditional way. The Mezcaloteca only serves mezcals that satisfy its strict selection criteria and comply with the traditional craft and flavors of the spirit's native region.

The basic steps of mezcal production are always the same: the hearts of the agave plant are harvested, roasted in a pit (palenque) in the ground, crushed, allowed to naturally ferment, and then distilled. A mezcal will always be at least 45% alcohol by volume. Depending on how long it has been aged, a mezcal will have either joven, reposado, or añejo added to its name. When a maestro mezcalero begins producing a batch of mezcal, it is because the spirit is intended for a celebration, a ritual, or a banquet in the local community. This means that some of the mezcal is always drunk where it is made, rather than being put on sale. Every mezcal is a limited edition, unique, and impossible to replicate. To guarantee this level of quality, the traditional mezcals stocked by the Mezcaloteca all display the name of their place of origin and of the maestro mezcalero who made them.

DESTILADOS DE AGAVE
Y MEZCALES TRADICIONALES
DE
**LA MEZCALOTECA**

Sociedad Mexicana para la Conservación y Difusión
de Destilados de Agave y Mezcales Tradicionales, A.C.

**WWW.LAMEZCALOTECA.COM**

Reforma No. 506, Col. Centro, Oaxaca de Juárez,
Oaxaca C.P. 68000          RFC LM101010A

| | |
|---|---|
| Maestro Mezcalero | *Juan Vázquez* |
| Estado | *Oaxaca* |
| Población | *Miahuatlán* |
| Maguey(es) empleado(s) | *Tobala* |
| | *(agave potatorum)* |
| Tipo de horno | *Horno cónico de tierra* |
| Tipo de molienda | *Molino de piedra* |
| Tipo de tina de fermentación | *Madera de sabino* |
| Tipo de destilador | *Alambique de cobre* |
| Número de destilaciones | *2* |
| Ajuste de la riqueza alcohólica | *Puntas y corazón* |
| Fecha de destilación | *Mayo 2010* |
| Riqueza alcohólica | *52% Alc. Vol.* |
| Litros producidos | *200 L* |
| Lote | *.05-10* |
| Número de botella | *.01/100* |
| Cont. Net. | *750 mL* |
| Marca comercial | *A punto de Verona* |
| Número de socio | *.00010* |

ENVASADO DE ORIGEN
EL ABUSO EN EL CONSUMO DE ESTE PRODUCTO ES NOCIVO PARA LA SALUD

154

# CLASE AZUL
# AÑEJO TEQUILA

**Distillery · Clase Azul Spirits**
**Type · Tequila Añejo**

Clase Azul's tequilas begin in the highlands of Jalisco with mature Weber Blue agave, cooked for three days in traditional brick ovens: the juice is then crushed out, fermented, and distilled twice for the highest purity. Yet what sets Clase Azul apart are the intricate decanters, handmade by the local artisanal community. The Plata comes in a blue-accented clear glass bottle, the Reposado in a hand-painted white ceramic vessel; finally, the Azul Añejo decanters marry the indigenous Mexican clay with European glazing techniques, using precious metals including platinum, silver, and gold.

Alc/Vol: 40%
Location: Jesús Maria, Mexico
Established: 2001

## SUERTE
## TEQUILA BLANCO

Distillery · Tequilera Simbolo
Type · Tequila Blanco

Coloradans Laurence Spiewak and Lance Sokol do things a little differently with their line of Suerte Tequilas, preserving some traditional methods while pushing other old customs into the present. In Jalisco, the agave is slow-cooked in a brick oven and crushed using a giant stone wheel; the Blanco rests for two months in stainless steel tanks before bottling, while the Reposado, Añejo, and EXTRA Añejo are aged in white oak whiskey barrels for up to five years. In color gradations from clear to amber, the preparation brings out different notes, from citrus and herbs to oaken honey and vanilla.

## ARTENOM SELECCIÓN DE
## 1146 AÑEJO

Distillery · Las Joyas del Agave
Type · Tequila Añejo

Las Joyas del Agave celebrates the regional specificity of the Blue Weber agave from Atotonilco el Alto with its 1146 Añejo, made at 1,689 meters above sea level. Cultivated by Arquitecto Enrique Fonseca, a fifth-generation farmer and master distiller, the agave grown at that elevation offers a drier taste and complexity. The tequila is aged in French oak barrels for two to three years and then married and stored in American white oak bourbon barrels for an additional year. This process produces the desired balance of nutty, creamy, and spicy flavors, with notes of almond, caramel, and vanilla.

## CASA DRAGONES
## JOVEN SIPPING TEQUILA

Distillery · Destilería Leyros
Type · Tequila Joven

Casa Dragones is run by Bertha González Nieves, the first woman to hold the title of maestra tequilera, and Bob Pittman, one of the founders of MTV. They make just one product—Casa Dragones Joven Sipping Tequila. It is distilled in small batches and has been specifically designed to be enjoyed neat. Before bottling, the unaged silver tequila is blended with a secret quantity of extra aged tequila. This produces a rare style of 100% blue agave joven tequila. Its unique taste has earned it a great deal of praise among connoisseurs.

Alc/Vol: 40%
Location: Atotonilco El Alto, Mexico
Established: 2012

Alc/Vol: 40%
Location: Atotonilco El Alto, Mexico
Established: 1954

Alc/Vol: 40%
Location: Tequila, Mexico
Established: 2008

Gin
160

Destilerías
Xoriguer
171

Four Pillars
175

Monkey 47
176

Preussische
Spirituosen
Manufaktur Berlin
182

# The Berry Started It

•

In the sixteenth century, resourceful pharmacists in Belgium and Holland added the small fruits of the common juniper to a traditional grain distillate that was sold as medicine. The Dutch introduced the drink to the British, who were immediately smitten, rechristened it "gin", and sent it out into the world with their army and navy.

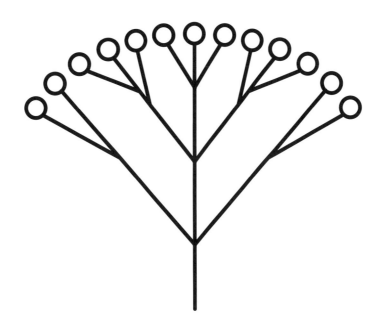

# Gin

•

A classic spirit with a checkered past. From a standard flavored
brandy to a boom in recent years, it's been quite a journey for gin.
An unprecedented career that, with few exceptions,
has only gone uphill.

The gin we know and love today has a history more varied and
dynamic than that of any other spirit. Drinks such as rum, aquavit,
whiskey, cognac, and absinthe have been produced in largely
the same way—at least in terms of the basic techniques and recipes—ever since they were invented. If, however, we look at the
evolution of gin, we find that its composition, distillation, and sensory properties (among other things) have rarely stood still over
the past 800 years.

The history of juniper-berry spirits, and therefore of gin, begins much earlier than most origin legends claim—namely in the
medieval monasteries of Central and Southern Europe. There, in
addition to wormwood, anise, fennel, and caraway (cf. absinthe
and aquavit), the highly aromatic fruit of the juniper bush and its
essential oils were used to flavor poor-quality spirits. The juniper
masked the bad-tasting ingredients and made the drink palatable.
This was, therefore, an early version of a juniper spirit.

Around 1650, Dr. Franz de la Boë, a professor of medicine at
Leiden University in the Netherlands, developed the recipe for the
original genever (also known as jenever), an alcoholic beverage
intended for commercial consumption and made, partly, by distilling juniper berries (Flemish: jeneverbes; Latin: Juniperus com-
munis). The drink had an extremely positive effect on the mood,
which quickly made it a hit with the people. It achieved great
popularity throughout the Dutch provinces, became one of the
first high-proof drugs available to the masses, and was even used
as a way of raising morale among the troops of the royal Dutch
armed forces.

English sailors got to experience the effects of the drink
during the Anglo-Dutch Wars, when the two countries fought for
supremacy of the world's oceans. The only way the English could
make sense of the brutal, brave, and self-sacrificing combat of the
hopelessly outnumbered Dutch soldiers was by believing it was
the result of their magic potion—i.e. the generous rations of genever
doled out on Dutch warships. As the legend spread, so the English
sailors started adapting the recipe for what had come to be known

as "Dutch courage". When they returned home, they brought the idea for their own genever with them.

In early eighteenth-century Britain, thanks in large part to William of Orange, a Dutch king on the English throne, "genever" was quickly shorted to "gin" and proceeded to take every layer of society by storm. By 1736, Britain was producing six times as much gin as beer—though at the time any distilled spirit was called gin. The situation escalated into such a craze that, during one fateful summer in the second half of the eighteenth century, all the grain harvested in London and the surrounding area was used for gin. With nothing left to make bread, many people faced starvation.

In 1740, during one of the first peaks in the period known as the Gin Craze, Britain's consumption of gin increased to such a phenomenal degree that King George II stepped in. He passed several laws designed to limit the drinking and sale of gin, and forced gin makers to guarantee a better-quality spirit so as to improve public health. Other gin acts followed, however, as did a number of periods in which gin making was banned outright.

All this happened at a time when drinking badly made spirits was a safer choice than consuming the filthy water from the Thames (which, incidentally, suggests a parallel with absinthe's heyday in late nineteenth century Paris).

Around 1761, Old Tom Gin, which contained sugar and various botanicals, conquered the market. The flavors, particularly the sugar, were only intended to mask the unpleasant taste of the low-grade spirit that was used to make Old Tom. Progressive

distilleries saw the potential of a high-quality alcoholic drink and set about improving the recipes.

No one knows for sure which manufacturers were the first to come up with the gin recipes that roughly correspond to the drink as it exists today. What we do know is that the column still (with concentrator), which was invented by Aeneas Coffey, an Irishman, around 1831, was a major step towards achieving a much cleaner, "dry" gin—one that did not have an aftertaste of grain or wine-based spirits. Today, the name London dry gin can only be used for genuine distillates that are flavored by macerating botanicals. Industrial gins made using essences and artificial flavors (a process known as cold compounding) cannot call themselves by that name. That said, the term is widely misused within the global alcohol industry.

## Modern-day Gin

In the 1860s, Jerry Thomas, a progressive and creative barkeeper from San Francisco, realized that gin had the potential to improve his business. He thus set about introducing a variety of cocktails—Martinez, Gin Sling, Tom Collins, Gin Fizz—that are still famous today. But these concoctions were merely the vanguard of the Gin & Tonic, one of the most successful mixed drinks the world has ever seen. It owes its existence to the discovery of a compound contained in the bark of the South American cinchona tree (known as quina-quina or "the bark of barks" in Quechua). The compound,

quinine, was found to have effective antimalarial properties—and with malaria wiping out large numbers of British colonial troops in Southeast Asia, people began wondering how to get the extremely bitter quinine into a form palatable enough for the soldiers to consume.

British drinks company Schweppes came up with the inspired solution: Indian Tonic Water, a fizzy drink containing quinine that went on sale around the world in 1870. The drink quickly became a hit during Britain's colonial campaigns in India and East Asia. It was especially popular when mixed with gin to make the glorious mixed drink that is still a firm favorite today.

The triumph of the G&T in the British colonies and the increasing ease with which it was possible to access exotic spices changed the way gin was made. Manufacturers adapted and expanded the ingredients to reflect the now-widespread pairing with tonic water. An increasing number of exotic herbs and spices were added to the traditional genever recipe and this changed the complexities of the gin's taste. The end of the nineteenth century can thus be considered as the birth of modern gin, a spirit that would help British drinking culture fly high again.

In 1896, Thomas Stuart invented the true Dry Martini at The Savoy Hotel in London. Other famous cocktails, such as the Singapore Sling (1915) and the Gin Gimlet (1928), were not far behind. After that, however, things quietened down on the gin front. Prohibition, the Wall Street Crash and, not least, the Second World War, kept the demand for cocktails low. Until, that is, a certain Bond, James Bond, ordered a Vodka Martini in Dr. No. It might have been a cheap, inferior version of the original, but it was also extremely successful. This was one of the first and most lucrative examples of product placement in a film. If you look closely, you can easily tell which vodka brand was behind this gambit which, while undeniably brilliant, was the beginning of a somewhat darker chapter in the history of bar culture.

## Another Gin Craze

In the 1990s, though, gin was back on everyone's lips. Slowly but surely, it began fighting its way back to the top of the clear-spirit pile. Many large manufacturers initially became trademarks of the international bar culture—and this despite the fact that their industrial products no longer had much in common with true distillates. Most were produced using cold compounding, in which essential oils are added "cold" to ethyl alcohol. The results were cheap and one-dimensional, but their popularity meant that true hand-distilled, aromatic gins had all but died out by the start of the twenty-first century.

Craft distillers were, therefore, not at all interested in gin at first. That all changed very abruptly in 2008, though, when a few small distilleries—mostly in Germany and the U.K.—began returning to the crafts of macerating, percolating, and distilling natural ingredients known as botanicals to produce new, highly aromatic, and properly distilled gins. The first stars of the New Western Style Gin scene (I am not exactly sure how we are supposed to understand "Western" here) did more than just catch the attention of the global bar scene and drinks aficionados—they also prompted an incredible boom within both the spirits industry and the craft distillery movement. Thousands of new gins sprung up all over the world, with some taking a more traditional approach and others trying out entirely new flavors and ingredients. (Christoph Keller)

## PARLOUR GIN

**Distillery · Eau Claire Distillery**
**Type · London Dry Gin**

Eau Claire Distillery is located just outside Calgary in a building that dates back to the 1920s and was once used as a movie theater, a center for local politics, and a dancehall. The distillery chose the name "Parlour" as a nod to the days when most socializing happened in these dedicated reception rooms. Locally grown barley is mixed with tried-and-tested gin ingredients such as juniper, coriander, and orange peel. North American saskatoon berries, rosehip, and a little ginger spice also feature. This unusual combination is definitely a conversation starter.

Alc/Vol: 40%
Location: Turner Valley (AB), Canada
Established: 2014

## BROKEN HEART GIN

**Distillery · Broken Heart Spirits**
**Type · London Dry Gin**

Broken Heart Gin is the poignant epilogue to a story of a friendship between Joerg Henkenhaf and Bernd Schnabel, two German distillers living in New Zealand: after Schnabel's untimely passing, Henkenhaf collaborated with Schnabel's partner to commemorate him in the form of a spirit he loved to make. The gin itself has a crisp palate, with lemony and rosemary notes, based on spring water and a blend of eleven organic botanicals. Produced at Joerg's Cromwell distillery and sold in beautifully designed bottles with a trompe l'oeil label, the gin has also earned international awards—a true labor of love.

Alc/Vol: 40%
Location: Arrowtown, New Zealand
Established: 2012

## NB GIN

**Distillery · NB Distillery Limited**
**Type · London Dry Gin**

NB Gin reflects Steve and Viv Muir's mixture of stubborn adherence to tradition, fond embrace of eccentricity, and pursuit of exceptional quality at any cost. Their home on the East Lothian coast has developed into a ginnery and laboratory, where pure British grain spirit and exactly seven botanicals are infused in a copperhead still, one pipe displaying a peculiar kink. Small batches of no more than 100 litres are made at a time, all blended, bottled, and labeled by hand. The gin has won accolades from global experts, including eighth-generation gin maker Charles Maxwell of Thames Distillers.

Alc/Vol: 42%
Location: North Berwick, United Kingdom
Established: 2013

## KUR GIN

Distillery · Wildwood Spirits Co.
Type · London Dry Gin

Erik Liedholm is an accredited sommelier and has also completed a master distilling program. Rather than being all about the dry theory, though, he mainly uses his head to come up with practical recipes for prizewinning spirits. His distillery in Bothell, Washington State, sources 90 percent of the ingredients for its gin and vodka from nearby farms. Kur, a gin modeled on London dry gin, spent 2014 scooping up one gold medal after the other. It is made using red Washington wheat that emphasizes the juniper notes and the flavors that come from Seville oranges and the apples grown in Liedholm's garden. Although the law prevents distillers from claiming their liquor is beneficial for your health, the name of this gin (pronounced "cure") reveals that a sip or two will do you a world of good.

Alc/Vol: 40%
Location: Bothell (WA), USA
Established: 2013

## SIPSMITH
## LONDON DRY GIN

Distillery · Sipsmith Distillery
Type · London Dry Gin

Sipsmith's classic London dry gin uses ten carefully selected botanicals from around the world—Macedonian juniper, Bulgarian coriander, Belgian angelica, Italian orris root, Chinese cassia bark, Madagascan cinnamon, and Spanish licorice, ground almond, orange, and lemon peel. The distilling takes place in Prudence, London's first new copper still in 200 years, a bespoke design combining a pot, carter head, and common still. Sipsmith's sloe gin, however, goes through an extra step, resting on wild sloe berries over the winter months to achieve a balanced sweetness with hints of cassis.

Alc/Vol: 29%
Location: London, United Kingdom
Established: 2008

## SIDERIT
## DRY GIN

Distillery · Destilería Siderit
Type · London Dry Gin

Not for nothing is Spain considered the place where the rediscovery of Gin & Tonic culture began. The spirit does not always have to be imported from abroad, as more and more local producers are entering the market. One example of this is Gin Siderit. Distilled in a filigree glass column, the gin is based on a recipe that mixes a rye distillate with numerous herbs, fruits, and spices, such as Spanish almonds, Jamaican hibiscus, and pink pepper. This is a great gin, and no doubt the hippest bars of Barcelona, Ibiza, and Madrid have already found the perfect tonic to accompany it.

Alc/Vol: 43%
Location: Cantabria, Spain
Established: 2013

## ADLER
## BERLIN DRY GIN

Distillery · Preussische Spirituosen
Manufaktur
Type · Dry Gin

Adler Berlin Dry Gin is based on a fine wheat distillate aged for six months and a recipe that allows the juniper berries to define the spirit's sensory impressions. The subtle composition of the spice blend—lavender and orange blossom, masterwort root, ginger, coriander, angelica seeds, valerian root, lemon peel, hop cones, elecampane root, allspice, abelmoschus grains, and anacyclus root—carries the aroma of the juniper berries and allows the taste to linger. The two-stage distillation process happens in a vacuum still that was made by brothers Daniel & Kluge in Reinickendorf, Berlin, in 1952. Once distilled, the gin spends three to six months in stoneware containers that are over 100 years old. This achieves a perfect balance of the gin's aromas.

## REISETBAUER
## BLUE GIN

Distillery · Reisetbauer Qualitätsbrand
Type · Dry Gin

When it comes time to harvest the fruits of his 13,000 Williams pear trees, Hans Reisetbauer camps out as his distillery. Pears are just one of the many types of fruit that he turns into award-winning spirits close to Linz in Austria. Even so, people say that his intuition for the perfect distillation time is so strong that it stays with him even when he is asleep. To fill the quieter period between harvests at the start of the year, Reisetbauer developed a dry gin. It is based on Mulan wheat grown in Upper Austria and gently distilled three times in a pot still. Before the third round, the 27 botanicals from 14 countries are macerated. They lend the gin a fresh, citrusy, peppery flavor that is so good it even won an award in the birthplace of gin.

## MARDER GIN

Distillery · Brennerei Marder
Edelbrände
Type · Dry Gin

The Marder distillery, which lies in the south of the Black Forest and is now into its third generation, does not participate in competitions: "We've already won everything there is to win," says Edmund Marder. His son Stefan is now at the helm of the family business and, since launching a Marder gin, has started a new chapter at the fruit-focused distillery. It took him a year and a half of testing and more than 80 attempts to get the spirit just right. The end result is a clean, 43% dry gin that is distilled several times over and enriched with spring water. The gin's juniper side is somewhat understated and allows fresh, citrusy bergamot flavors to come to the fore. Lavender dominates the palate, giving way to licorice at the finish.

Alc/Vol: 42%
Location: Berlin, Germany
Established: 1874

Alc/Vol: 40%
Location: Axberg, Austria
Established: 1994

Alc/Vol: 43%
Location: Albbruck-Unteralpfen, Germany
Established: 1953

# HERNÖ
# NAVY STRENGTH GIN

Distillery · Hernö Gin Distillery
Type · Dry Gin

Navy strength gin is traditionally 57% alcohol by volume. At that strength, sailors could easily test whether their daily gin ration had been watered down too much. The men would sprinkle some gin onto gunpowder and put a flame to it. If the powder ignited, it meant the gin was good. Hernö Gin is made using eight botanicals, all of which are certified organic: juniper berries from Hungary, coriander seeds from Bulgaria, hand-peeled lemons, lingonberries from Sweden, meadowsweet from the U.K., black pepper from India, cassia from Indonesia, and fresh vanilla from Madagascar. The higher alcohol content of Hernö Navy Strength Gin really brings out the best in its carefully selected ingredients.

Alc/Vol: 57%
Location: Dala, Sweden
Established: 2011

# JENSEN'S
# BERMONDSEY DRY GIN

Distillery · Bermondsey Distillery
Type · Dry Gin

Christian Jensen discovered vintage gin on a business trip to Japan, when he was still working full time as an IT expert. He enjoyed it so much that he decided to try and make his own. Back home in London, he started tinkering with recipes and doing research until he finally achieved the balanced juniper flavor and perfectly silky texture found in the gins of the 1920s. After that, he thought he would just kick back at home and enjoy gin martinis made exactly as he wanted them. But news of his knack for the drink soon spread and Jensen began supplying other gin lovers. He has been making his Bermondsey Dry Gin since 2004, using custom-made distillation equipment housed beneath the brick railway arches of the London neighborhood that gave the gin its name.

Alc/Vol: 57%
Location: Dala, Sweden
Established: 2011

167

## GIN EVA

Distillery · Eva's Distillery
Type · Dry Gin

Being an Erasmus student does not necessarily have to mean a year of binge drinking and broken hearts. Quite the opposite can happen, in fact. When Eva Maier Gomez, who hails from Barcelona, came to Geisenheim, Germany, to expand her oenological knowledge, she fell head over heels for Stefan Winterling, the son of a vintner. Their love for viticulture and each other took them to Mallorca in 2008, where they both got the urge to experiment with making their own gin. They use ingredients found on the island, such as a fragrant and slightly salty juniper from the Es Trenc dunes. Local citrus fruits and herbs are macerated for a long time to give the dry gin its intensive aroma. Stefan must have earned himself a lot of brownie points when he decided to name the gin after his wife and put a photo of her grandmother on the label.

Alc/Vol: 45%
Location: Llucmajor, Spain
Established: 2012

## VICTORIA GIN

Distillery · Victoria Spirits
Type · Dry Gin

Victoria Gin features a youthful Queen Victoria on its medicine-like bottle, a reference to Victoria Spirits' fresh approach to tradition. Handmade in small batches in a wood-fired, German copper pot still, the Victoria Gin unites wild-gathered botanicals in a drink that parallels the complexity of single-malt whiskey. Bottling only the "hearts", or the middle of each run, Victoria Spirits ensures the utmost quality in their production. The Vancouver Island distillery is also carbon-neutral, combining distiller Peter Hunt's technological knowhow with sustainable energy and production systems.

Alc/Vol: 45%
Location: Victoria (BC), Canada
Established: 2008

## PREMIUM GIN BATCH NO. 2

Distillery ·
East London Liquor Company
Type · Dry Gin

Like any good boyband, the five craftsmen behind the East London Liquor Company have every type covered and each bring their own brand of coolness to the table. They recently came up with what sounds like a picture-perfect business idea: open a distillery and bar in a disused glue factory in London's East End, where no new distillery has opened in more than a century. The East London Liquor Company now serves its own handcrafted gin, rum, vodka, and whiskey, as well as craft beers sourced from external suppliers. Its 47% Premium Gin Batch 2 is made using British wheat and, thanks to a bouquet of the finest herbs in the form of angelica root, lavender, sage, and winter savory, it delivers a boldly herbaceous yet well-balanced flavor.

Alc/Vol: 47%
Location: London, United Kingdom
Established: 2012

## ATALAY GIN
## DER SIEDLER

Distillery · Schultz´ens Siedlerhof
& Whiskydestillerie
Type · Dry Gin

"I don't think it's just that I've found something that I can do. I think I was really born
to do this," says Atalay Aktas, who grew up
in Kreuzberg, Berlin, as the son of Turkish
immigrants. These days, he runs a cocktail
bar in what used to be an old pub in his
neighborhood. As a child, Aktas would try
anything and everything (including dish
soap) to see what it tasted like. It was this
fascination for flavors (combined with his
charm) that won him the title of Germany's
Best Bartender in 2013. Aktas teamed up
with Michael Schultz, the head of a family-run business making wine and fruit
brandies west of Berlin, to create a limited
edition of Schultz's Siedler Gin. The result,
Atalay Gin, features Slovenian mountain
juniper, lemon peel, rose, and lavender,
topped off with coriander and cardamom.
Icelandic glacier water is used to bring the
gin down to drinking strength.

Alc/Vol: 47 %
Location: Werder, Germany
Established: 2004

## HALF HITCH
## GIN

Distillery · Holdsworth Spirits & Company
Type · Dry Gin

Camden Town is best known today for
its sprawling markets, goths, punks, and
boozers, but within its past there also lies
a tradition of gin distilling, as discovered
by local Mark Holdsworth. A half-centu-
ry since the last gin production in Camden
Lock, he has launched Half Hitch—a reference to a rope knot used for mooring
barges—to revive the tradition amidst the
industrial warehouses and canals. Half
Hitch Gin combines a modern vacuum distillation of Malawian black tea, Calabrian
bergamot, and English wood, pepper, and
hay, with copper pot still gin from Langley's
Distillery in the Midlands.

Alc/Vol: 40 %
Location: London , United Kingdom
Established: 2014

## ROCK ROSE
## GIN

Distillery · Dunnet Bay Distillery
Type · Dry Gin

Over 1,000 years ago, Vikings harvested
Rhodiola Rosea from the cliffs of the northern Scottish highlands to gain strength
for their sea voyages. Today, this plant
gives Rock Rose Gin its name: Dunnet Bay
Distillery blends the aromatic root with
two kinds of juniper—for depth and lemony notes—and other botanicals including
local Rowan, sea buckthorn, and blaeber-
ries. The gin is produced as a one-shot distillation in "Elizabeth", a John Dore copper pot still with botanical vapor infusion
basket, using the water of St. Johns Loch.
Each batch produces up to 700 bottles of
truly Caithness gin.

Alc/Vol: 41.5 %
Location: Dunnet, United Kingdom
Established: 2014

## HELSINKI DRY GIN

Distillery ·
The Helsinki Distilling Company
Type · Dry Gin

Kai Kilpinen and Mikko Mykkänen, two Finns with wonderfully alliterative names, teamed up with their Irish friend Séamus Holohan to embark on an experiment. The trio share the same sense of humor and a passion for whiskey and gin—although the latter probably also applies to the majority of the adult Finnish population. In any case, the group quit their jobs to set up a distillery in Helsinki and try their hands at a Nordic gin. The result contains Balkan juniper berries, Mediterranean lemons, Seville oranges, and the Arctic lingonberry (one of eight spices), which survives the distillation process and gives the gin its Nordic note. The team are also planning to add a bar to the distillery and a sauna that will be housed in an old chimney stack, warmed by heat produced during the distillation process.

Alc/Vol: 47 %
Location: Helsinki, Finland
Established: 2013

## GIN XORIGUER MAHON

Distillery · Destilerías Xoriguer
Type · Dry Gin

Gin found its way onto Menorca in the eighteenth century. British soldiers and sailors stationed on the island could not stand to be apart from their beloved national drink, so locals set up distilleries to supply the demand. By importing juniper berries and using wine alcohol as a basis, they came up with a Spanish interpretation of gin. While the British knocked it back, the locals fell in love with it and made it part of every wedding, christening, and funeral held on the island. Miguel Pons Justo launched the Xoriguer brand in 1945 and helped the drink gradually find an audience outside of Menorca. Gin Xoriguer, which is sold in traditional brandy jars, is still owned by the Pons family. As long as it stays that way, the secret of the botanicals will remain under lock and key.

Alc/Vol: 38 %
Location: Mahón, Spain
Established: 1945

# Destilerías Xoriguer

When the British Royal Navy invaded the Balearic island of Menorca in 1708, its sailors crowded into the port bars demanding gin. Back home, gin had long since replaced brandy as the intoxicant of choice and had sent the whole of England into a collective frenzy that had become known as the Gin Craze.

Confirming the principle of supply and demand, traders on the island started trying to work out how they could quickly get their hands on large quantities of cheap gin and make their business relationships with the members of the Royal Navy as profitable as possible. The simplest and most lucrative solution was to make the spirit themselves. There was, however, one problem: Menorca's climate meant that no juniper grew on the island. Imports from regions around the Pyrenees quickly proved to be the solution and it was not long before Menorca was home to numerous flourishing distilleries. They based their gins on local alcohol made from grapes, which lent the drink a fruity flavor that proved as popular with the locals as it did with the British target group. Gin quickly became part of the island's drinking culture, especially as a refreshing punch made with lemons and oranges. Nowadays, there is only one family-run, artisan gin producer left on the island: Xoriguer. The brand's label displays a windmill called Xoriguer that was built by the Pons family in 1784. Milling was the family business for many years until Miguel Pons Justo decided to change careers and become a distiller in the early twentieth century. The Pons family gin is fruity with bold juniper notes. The recipe is a well-guarded secret, and only certain family members know what botanicals give the gin its aroma. Once it has been distilled in traditional wood-fired copper stills, the gin is stored in oak casks and then bottled in either earthenware jars or bottles featuring a small handle. The labels with the eye-catching windmill logo are applied by hand.

| NAVY STRENGTH GIN | BARREL AGED GIN |
|---|---|

**Distillery · Four Pillars**
**Type · Dry Gin**

**Distillery · Four Pillars**
**Type · Dry Gin**

The Olympic ethos that says "it's not the winning but the taking part that counts" definitely does not apply to Cameron MacKenzie, a talented Australian entrepreneur with a keen sporting spirit. He might have failed to win a medal in the 400-meter relay in Atlanta, but, 17 years later, he took a double gold for his first gin at the San Francisco World Spirits Competition. The win is all the more impressive given that the Four Pillars distillery in the Yarra Valley has only been up and running since 2013. The business has made an alcohol expert out of MacKenzie, who was all but teetotal in his sporting days. His cherished copper still, Wilma, recently produced a navy strength gin that contains organic oranges and fresh Byron Bay finger limes. This unusual citrus fruit underscores the Asian spices of star anise and coriander, while turmeric adds an earthy quality and a freshness not too far removed from cucumber. The gin is juicy yet clean—and it has just picked up another award for the distillery, this time in Hong Kong.

Cameron MacKenzie, Stuart Gregor, and Matt Jones the founders of this Australian distillery, say that the four pillars of their gin are: 1) Wilma, their German-made copper still; 2) the naturally filtered water from the Yarra Valley; 3) Asian spices, Australian botanicals, and Mediterranean oranges; 4) a little bit of love. That last one is very much present in their limited-edition Barrel Aged Gin. Made using a solera system of nine oak barrels connected by tubes, the gin enters into a marriage of sorts. After it has aged for a certain amount of time, it is mixed with a younger gin. The end result comes out at 43.8% and shines with nutmeg, cinnamon, vanilla, and the citrus character of preserved kumquat and orange aromas. Cam suggests keeping things simple and enjoying it over a single ice cube with a drop of honey.

Alc/Vol: 58.8%
Location: Yarra Valley, Australia
Established: 2013

Alc/Vol: 43.8%
Location: Yarra Valley, Australia
Established: 2013

# Four Pillars

Strictly speaking, Cameron MacKenzie and his friend Stuart Gregor are wine people. The two Australians have spent years making, selling, or writing about wine. But they are also fans of gin, which is not really surprising given that British culture still has a tangible influence on Australia today. "As gin drinkers, we wanted to make great tonic," says MacKenzie, explaining how they ended up founding the Four Pillars distillery. "But the discussion rapidly moved to gin. It took us three years to launch after making that decision." A third man, Matt Jones, joined the team during the planning phase. The first batch of Four Pillars Gin arrived in 2013, made in a 450-liter still affectionately named Wilma. MacKenzie, Gregor, and Jones currently do their distilling in the Yarra Valley, where their small company sublets space on a winery. But with demand for gin so high in Australia—as it is in many other countries—they are planning to move premises and expand production in 2015.

"We're not making London dry gin. We love London dry, but we're a very long way from London. Our goal was to make a modern Australian gin," says MacKenzie, before going on to list the ingredients that make Four Pillars Gin such a delicious mix of cultures. As well as the traditional ingredients, they feature exotic Australian additions such as lemon myrtle and the leaves of the Tasmanian pepperberry. The distillery's Navy Strength Gin is an extra spicy, overproof number that contains ginger, turmeric, and Australian finger limes. The term Navy Strength is said to come from the days when captains of the British Royal Navy were especially keen to have good-quality gin onboard as they travelled the high seas. To check whether a gin was up to scratch, they would sprinkle a little onto some gunpowder and set it on fire. If the powder burned, the gin was good to go. From the looks of it, MacKenzie and his friends are having a whole lot of fun doing the job that grew out of a rekindled passion for gin.

# Monkey 47

Thanks to these two men, the Black Forest is now associated with more than just cuckoo clocks, gateaux, and a heavy sense of melancholy. With their Monkey 47 Schwarzwald Dry Gin, Alexander Stein and Christoph Keller have put this part of southern Germany well and truly on the world gin map. The handcrafted spirit, which contains 47 botanicals along with other fresh (and painstakingly selected) ingredients, has played a huge part in the gin boom that has recently swept Germany and many other countries. It has also set new standards by being one of very few gins flavorful enough to be enjoyed neat. The story begins back in 2008, when Keller, now Monkey 47's master distiller, had made a name for himself as a maker of fruit brandies. Having entered the business after switching careers,

Keller began sweeping up awards for the spirits he was making at the Stählemühle distillery near Lake Constance. One day he got an "oddball" call from Alexander Stein, the son of a Stuttgart brandy dynasty. Stein had spent several years abroad, working as a manager at Nokia, but now he wanted to get back to his roots. He told Keller a crazy story about a British Air Force pilot, Montgomery Collins, who pitched up in the Black Forest in the fifties and opened a guesthouse called The Wild Monkey. During his time there, Collins devised a special gin recipe, which Stein and Keller discovered and used as the blueprint for Monkey 47. In doing so, they created probably the best-tasting Anglo-Southern German union imaginable.

# MONKEY 47
# SCHWARZWALD DRY GIN

**Distillery · Black Forest Distillers**
**Type · New Western Dry Gin**

Top dog in Germany's current gin boom is actually a monkey made of 47 fine ingredients, including a variety of herbs, fruits, and spices. Monkey 47 first saw the light of day about a decade ago in Stählemühle, a fruit brandy distillery located in the south of Germany and highly respected in the distilling scene. Over the years, the spirit has grown so much that it is now more of a powerful silverback than a cute little lap monkey. The gin is a Black Forest success story and shows how a handcrafted product with a gutsy story and an eye-catching brand can revolutionize the gin market.

Alc/Vol: 47 %
Location: Eigeltingen, Germany
Established: 2009

# GIN SUL

**Distillery · Altonaer Spirituosen Manufaktur**
**Type · New Western Dry Gin**

Stephan Garbe's eyes still sparkle every time he sees steam rising from the small, perfectly polished still in Hamburg's Altona district. "When Sunday comes around, I can't wait for the week to begin again," says Garbe, who used to work in advertising. The idea for the business came to him during a period of reflection on Portugal's Costa Vicentina. All along the rocky coastline he found masses of wild juniper berries growing right alongside fragrant gum rockroses. The flowers now appear in Gin Sul and, paired with lemons from the western Algarve, are responsible for creating its unique taste. The spirit is distilled slowly and in small batches. The macerate, which is produced from the botanicals, alcohol, and water from Lüneburg Heath, is gasified and passed through a basket of lemon rind, rosemary, and rose petals. When the gin is ready and waiting in its white ceramic bottles, Garbe himself goes out to deliver it to his buyers.

Alc/Vol: 43 %
Location: Hamburg, Germany
Established: 2013

# THE DUKE
# MUNICH DRY GIN

Distillery · The Duke Destillerie
Type · New Western Dry Gin

Founded by Maximilian Schauerte and Daniel Schönecker, the Duke began as an experiment in a backyard in the center of Munich and has now developed into a bio-certified distillery. Their Munich Dry Gin is a handmade, organic gin with a twist: in addition to 13 traditional botanicals, the spirit acquires a unique Bavarian flavor from German hops and malt. These ingredients are macerated in an all-natural grain spirit, distilled twice at low temperatures in a copper still, and finally filtered for purity before bottling. The soft palate gives way to a sweet finish with a hint of coffee.

Alc/Vol: 45%
Location: Munich, Germany
Established: 2008

# MADAME GENEVA
# GIN ROUGE

Distillery · Kreuzritter
Type · New Western Dry Gin

You would never have guessed it, but the collaboration of a physician, a nutritionist, and a spirits expert in Münster had nothing to do with giving up a whiskey diet, but rather, with producing a whole repertoire of highly concentrated alcohols. And of course, with the question of taste above all. Using 46 botanicals, Madame Geneva Gin Rouge really put her palate to the test. An infusion of red wine from an old Apulian „primitivo" grapevine rounds out the tart, bitter and fresh notes, giving a gin and tonic a slightly disreputable touch, with juniper as its constant companion. By the way, Madame is no lightweight: the two-kilo bottles leave a big impression—and not just where taste is concerned.

Alc/Vol: 44.4%
Location: Mühlen, Germany
Established: 2005

# Preussische Spirituosen Manufaktur Berlin

•

Kaiser Wilhelm I set up a spirit-making institute to deal with surplus harvests and train distillers. The buildings later stood empty for many years and have had their share of financial woes. But now the Prussian copper stills are bubbling away again, just like in the good old days.

Faced with a surplus of crops from Brandenburg's farms, Kaiser Wilhelm I—or rather, his Prussian administrators—had to find an answer to a pressing question: what to do with all these potatoes? After all, surplus crops lead to unstable agricultural prices and the Prussians were very suspicious of instability. Their solution was to buy the potatoes in Berlin that could not be sold on the free market and turn them into alcohol. To ensure that everything was organized in the proper Prussian way, the state issued a cabinet order that founded the Versuchs- und Lehranstalt für Spiritusfabrikation (Research and Teaching Institute for the Manufacture of Spirits) in 1874. A well-respected professor, Max Delbrück, was tasked with leading the institute, which was located in the Berlin district of Wedding. In addition to overseeing the production of industrial alcohol, Delbrück was also responsible for the training of every new distiller in Germany. This was because Prussia was having a crisis of confidence: while other countries were producing world-class spirits with a long tradition, its own schnapps culture was limited to spirits and herbal liqueurs that got little international attention and were mainly used as medicines. The idea was that by doing research, developing recipes, and providing improved training—in other words, by making a state-decreed leap forward in quality—the institute would whip Germany's spirits industry into shape.

In 1874, the status of Berlin's urban development was such that the brick buildings of the newly established institute lay on the outermost edge of the city and had beautiful views of fields and lakes. The buildings were constructed with the latest technology and operated with Prussian thoroughness. Production at the institute flourished under the name Adler Spirituosen and hit its high point around the turn of the century. The big sellers were gin and vodka, German classics like caraway, corn, herbs, and a series of liqueurs based on recipes that Delbrück and his students developed over years of research.

When the First World War began, towever, crop surpluses became a thing of the past, and while hard liquor was in high demand among Berliners, the money necessary to buy it was in very short supply. The institute was thus forced to halt production. It was not until the 1950s that the Wedding location and its traditions were revived. Under a new, rather less memorable name—Institut für Gärungsgewerbe Berlin (Berlin Institute for Fermentation)—the old distillation rooms began producing gin and vodka again. However, none of the subsequent operators managed to match the successes of the past.

Today, the former research and teaching institute lies on one of Berlin's large, noisy thoroughfares. The internal and external damage caused by the Second World War was fixed during the fifties in a most utilitarian fashion. "Der Lack ist ab," as Berliners would say. The bloom is off the rose. Nevertheless, 2009 saw a new sign go up at the entrance that reads Preussische Spirituosen Manufaktur (Prussian Spirits Manufactory). A visit to the second floor reveals the old distillation equipment—stills, funnels, pressure gauges, pipes, filler valves—in all its copper glory. What was once state-of-the-art technology is now pure nostalgia. It is, however, very functional nostalgia that has been put back into service by two men with a shared vision: to revive the spirit of the recipes that have been so carefully handed down through the years.

When Ulf Stahl, a professor of engineering, and Gerald Schroff, a hotelier, skied into each other on a piste in Austria, they did not immediately become the best of friends. But when their paths happened to cross again that evening, this time in a hotel bar (the Berlin professor in front of it, the southern German hotelier behind it), they discovered they shared a passion for fine spirits. Stahl teaches at TU Berlin's microbiology department, which is located on the site of the former research and teaching institute in Wedding. The facility had stopped producing spirits shortly before the two men met, so it is not hard to imagine the rest of the story. Stahl and Schroff began distilling Adler gin and vodka again in 2005 and took over the entire factory in 2009.

The men behind the Preussische Spirituosen Manufaktur attach a great deal of importance to the traditions of the former institute. Only the best raw ingredients and their own mashes and distillates

go into the antique equipment. Complex processes and months of resting in antique stoneware containers make the spirits and liqueurs, which are now enjoying a revival, stand out from the crowd. Stahl and Schroff are especially pleased that the site is once again being used for teaching. Knowledge amassed over 150 years is now being passed on to distillers in masterclasses and advanced training courses.

# Famously Bitter

•

The bitterness of the herb known as Artemisia absinthium is responsible for giving two of the twentieth century's most fashionable drinks their defining characteristics. Absinthe and vermouth are now classics among spirits. As well as sharing the same basic ingredient, they also share the same fate: although they are widely known, it is not unusual for them to fall into relative obscurity for decades at a time. Until, that is, a new generation of spirits aficionados rediscovers its taste for bitterness.

# Absinthe

•

**A good absinthe is prepared slowly and enjoyed in small sips. To understand how such a sedate drink came to be associated with all things satanic, we take a look back at the history of the green spirit.**

Artemisia Absinthium, 585

One day, in late-nineteenth-century Paris, Alfred Jarry, revolutionary playwright and enfant terrible, was found winding his way through Montmartre dressed as a fairy. He did not, however, have quite the same grace one would normally expect from a dainty mythical creature. With his hands and face painted green, he hurtled along the narrow streets on his bike, firing his pistol instead of ringing his bell, all to pay homage to his beloved absinthe.

The herbal spirit made of wormwood, anise, and other ingredients originated in Switzerland. At the time of Jarry's performance, it had, within the space of 100 years, gone from being the drink of French soldiers returning home victorious from Algeria, to the favorite of the bourgeoisie and bohemian society, to the shelves of the many bars frequented by the working classes. Phylloxera, a vicious grapevine pest, had destroyed most of the wine harvest and led to an unprecedented surge in the popularity of cheap industrial alcohol. The absinthe that it was used to produce became a smash-hit in the impoverished neighborhoods of the city. It was incredibly cheap and an extremely effective way of giving the bleakness of daily life the run-around.

Wealthier members of French society also extensively cultivated the green hour, the period between 5 and 7 p.m. when they would enjoy a pick-me-up or two. At the same time, though, various temperance movements were claiming that absinthe was in league with death and the devil.

Mystifying stories of absinthe-fuelled excesses told of debauched orgies among artists and of utter madness, delirium, and murder. These tales, combined with the ban that was introduced in the early twentieth century, dialed up the fear factor, but also made the drink more desirable. Above all, though, absinthe consumption was the sign of a society that that was utterly addicted to alcohol. "You have to remember that people drank an incredible amount back then," says Hermann Plöckl, owner of the Absinth Depot in Berlin. "And the figures in France didn't even include wine," he adds. At 60 liters of pure alcohol per capita in 1913, the French were way, way ahead of everyone else.

In general, a marked enjoyment of absinthe has always been associated with French culture. "People like Oscar Wilde and his crowd drank it in England as a way of emulating the French way. It's like when someone smokes Gauloises cigarettes today because they want to feel like they're French," says David

Nathan-Maister, a British absinthe expert who has published his own encyclopedia on the drink.

In Switzerland, the birthplace of absinthe, the moralizing of the temperance movement eventually wore down the conscience of the people. After that, one murderer who—in addition to liters of wine—just happened to have drunk two glasses of absinthe was all it took for the 1908 referendum to come out clearly in favor of a ban on absinthe. In France, the First World War put an official end to people's enjoyment of the drink. "There were reports that French soldiers had gotten drunk and staged a mutiny. That made everyone panic, so they introduced a ban on absinthe. Incidentally, they did it on the same day as they banned croissants for using too much butter."

The ban was lifted in the 1990s. Since then, absinthe has been officially free to engage in its opalescent liaison with water once more. Nathan-Maister believes that the EU made an error

when it revised the rules on absinthe: products can now be sold that contain the same amount of thujone—the notorious neurotoxin of the wormwood plant—as the drink did a century ago. He does not think there will be a repeat of the earlier boom: "Absinthe will never be as popular as cognac, gin, or even rum. A lot of people don't like the aniseed flavor. You have to have had it as a child to really appreciate it." As for Hermann Plöckl, what he most appreciates about absinthe is the myth that surrounds it and, of course, its high quality. He is a big fan of the mood absinthe puts the drinker in: "It's a talkative drug—like cocaine and alcohol rolled into one."

Plöckl says that when the essential oils interact with the synapses, they cause the body to fully relax but keep the mind alert. He and Nathan-Maister both agree that the best place to find good absinthe is in the region where it was born: the Val-de-Travers in Switzerland and, just across the border, Pontarlier in France.

## EMPEROR NORTON ABSINTHE

Distillery · Raff Distillery
Type · Absinthe

Raff Distillerie was founded in 2011 by Carter Raff on Treasure Island, between San Francisco and Oakland, a few kilometers east of Alcatraz Island; he even fabricated the main production still, as well as a scale version for testing, from scratch. Raff's first release was the Emperor Norton Absinthe, named for a beloved nineteenth-century San Francisco eccentric. The absinthe begins with neutral brandy made from California grapes, and is then macerated with herbs and distilled, developing the characteristic vibrant green hue and the sweet licorice flavor.

Alc/Vol: 68%
Location: San Francisco (CA), USA
Established: 2011

## ADNAMS ABSINTHE ROUGE

Distillery · Adnams
Type · Absinthe

Adnams' Absinthe Rouge is so vividly, provocatively red that you could well imagine the devil himself emerging from the bottle and convincing whoever opened it to enter into a pact of the darkest variety. The spirit, which is made using an old French recipe, owes its ruby hue to the addition of hibiscus flowers, and its full-bodied flavor to anise, fennel, and coriander. John McCarthy, head distiller at Adnams, has won numerous awards for his gin and vodka—despite the distillery only being added to the long-standing brewery in 2010. His Absinthe Rouge has also been singled out for praise, winning a silver medal at the International Wine and Spirit Competition. Presumably the judges decided it was devilishly good stuff.

Alc/Vol: 66%
Location: Southwold, United Kingdom
Established: 2010

## ABSINTHE DU LAC DE CONSTANCE „KELLER ET FILS"

Distillery · Stählmühle
Type · Absinthe

Almost all of the absinthe produced nowadays doesn't have anything in common with the traditional absinthe from the nineteenth century. "Keller et Fils," the green fairy from Stählemühle in southern Germany, is different: It is based on the initial, authentic recipe and produced in accordance with the original procedure. The herbal ingredients such as Artemisia Absinthia, pontic vermouth, hyssop, melissa, or fennel are grown in their own herb garden. The ingredients are then harvested, dried, and immediately processed, guaranteeing a fresh, complex aroma. Describing the absinthe he developed over three years, Christoph Keller says it tastes like a "walk in a summery flower meadow in the mountains." Connoisseurs enjoy it straight and pure.

Alc/Vol: 68%
Location: Eigeltingen, Germany
Established: 2004

## ABSINTHE VERTE

Distillery · Leopold Bros.
Type · Absinthe

Leopold Bros. create their Absinthe Verte in the tradition of the great distillers of nineteenth-century Europe, beginning with a grape distillate base—in this case, Chilean pisco—and adding aniseed, fennel, grand wormwood, and other botanicals. The brilliant emerald green color is achieved by steeping the distillate in lemon balm and hyssop, while the fennel and wormwood build up a creamy, fruity palate. Made in a small batch copper still, the absinthe reflects the Leopold brothers' commitment to eco-brewing, using organic ingredients and efficient water systems to produce sustainable spirits.

## ARGALÀ
## PASTIS ARTIGIANALE

Distillery · Argalà
Type · Pastis

Enrico and Piero, two good-natured Italian friends, teamed up in 2011 to make a pastis. Enrico had his heart set on using a distillery in Roccavione that used to belong to his grandfather, so the pair got it up and running again. The main ingredients—anise and muscovado sugar—are both fair trade, and the herbs come from the valleys of Cuneo on the edge of the Maritime Alps. A few wild herbs from the surrounding area lend the pastis a unique flavor. When they had distilled their first batch, Enrico and Piero let their famiglia have a taste. The response was a resounding argalà, an expression of approval in Occitan that promptly became the name of the brand.

## TARQUIN'S HANDCRAFTED
## CORNISH PASTIS

Distillery · Southwestern Distillery
Type · Pastis

A playful pun on the local pastry, Tarquin's Cornish Pastis is the first British take on the French anise apéritif and has been swift to gain critical recognition for its fresh and invigorating flavor. The pastis begins with gorse flowers foraged on the blustery clifftops of Cornwall, combined with a variety of botanicals such as Turkish green aniseed, sweet fennel seeds, Chinese star anise, and Uzbek licorice root. A human touch guides every step, from pot distilling over a flame to filling and corking by hand, producing batches of up to 300 bottles of the silky-smooth pastis at a time.

Alc/Vol: 65%
Location: Denver (CO), USA
Established: 1999

Alc/Vol: 45%
Location: Roccavione, Italy
Established: 2011

Alc/Vol: 42%
Location: Cornwall, United Kingdom
Established: 2012

A copper pot still on the Cornish coast in the UK, where Southwestern Distillery is based and produces pastis and gin according to traditional techniques.

# La Hora del Vermú

•

**Italy of course and France, too, are the countries most commonly associated with the production and consumption of vermouth. What a lot of people do not know, however, is that vermouth also has a long tradition in Spain.**

Vermouth arrived in Spain via the Mediterranean—how else? Produced in Turin and shipped from Genoa, it was unloaded in Barcelona and traveled overland to Madrid. This was all thanks to the new industrial technology that had allowed brothers Luigi and Giuseppe Cora to expand their vermouth production (which had previously been done entirely by hand) to such an extent that exporting became a viable option in 1836. Vermouth was all the rage in Turin at the time. In 1786, a resourceful wine merchant called Antonio Benedetto Carpano had begun selling a fortified white wine sweetened with caramel, flavored with herbs, and designed to appeal to elegant Turin ladies. He named it after the German word for its most bitter ingredient, wormwood (Wermut). As well as proving popular with the good citizens of Turin, male and female, Carpano's creation also found favor with King Victor Amadeus III. This sealed Carpano's success, and vermouth became the aperitif of the hour in bars throughout Turin. Companies such as Cora, Cinzano, and Martini & Rossi soon introduced their own versions, and in no time at all Turin's economy became forever linked with the production of vermouth.

And so the joy of vermouth sloshed its way across the Mediterranean to Spain, where it was first embraced by fashion-conscious Spaniards and then by domestic wine merchants and producers. This led to a boom in new businesses in the Catalonian city of Reus. Situated in one of Spain's largest wine regions, Reus was already a flourishing center for the making and selling of wine and aguardiente. It was, therefore, more or less predestined to become home to the fashionable new drink. The first trademark for a vermouth was registered here in 1892. Not long after that, the area was home to 30 companies supplying the whole of Spain and fueling the growing trend.

Just as it was in Turin, vermouth was drunk as an aperitif in its new home. The reason lies in the ingredients, as the wormwood and other herbs and spices (anything from 30 to 150 different kinds) that are macerated in the wine are said to stimulate the appetite. The Ancient Greeks were also aware of these effects. They were

no strangers to mixing herbs with wine—though of course only for strictly medical purposes.

During the early twentieth century, Madrid and Barcelona in particular became home to countless bars, bodegas, and tabernas specializing in vermouth and vermouth-friendly tapas. The establishments ranged from small neighborhood bars that would get full to overflowing at aperitif time, to beautiful art nouveau temples catering to the wealthy middle classes. The most elegant of them all was surely Café Torino in Barcelona, sadly no longer there. Those who were lucky enough to frequent it nicknamed it— quite rightly—el Palacio del Vermú.

In Spain's heavily Catholic society, the hora del vermú, the time when people would gather for an aperitif after attending mass and before their traditionally late Sunday lunch, became part of the collective memory. People drank vermouth (over ice or with a splash of water), got together with friends and family, put the world to rights, flirted a little, and danced if the mood took them. The drink began to fall out of fashion in the seventies and eighties, when it had to make way for the likes of beer and gin. That did not, however, change the fact that entire generations of Spaniards had grown up in the glory days of the hora del vermú.

And now, it is back! The children and the children's children of the people who started this almost vanished tradition feel a nostalgic connection to vermouth, which is celebrating an unprecedented comeback, particularly in Barcelona and Madrid. In Reus, the few companies that managed to survive the slump have read the signs and upped their production. They have even opened a museum. Young winemakers and restaurateurs are digging out long-forgotten family recipes, setting up new vermouth labels, and opening vermouth bars. Top chefs are outdoing each other with tapas created specifically with the aperitif in mind. And people are even starting to dance again, to new music and the classics. Bienvenido a la hora del vermú!

# BORDIGA
# VERMUT BIANCO

Distillery · Bordiga Liquori
Type · Vermouth

Bordiga make their spirits "starting from the grass," in reference to their deep ties to agriculture in the Maira Valley. The distillery was founded in 1888 by Pietro Bordiga, whose success as a Turin bar owner inspired him to go to the source, high in the mountains. The white vermouth is still made according to the same recipe, using a waterbath distilling alembic heated on a wood fire to extract the botanical flavors to their fullest. The hand-drawn label, showing a robed man transporting the bottles by camel through an Arab landscape, refers to the blend of local herbs and exotic scents.

Alc/Vol: 18%
Location: Cuneo, Italy
Established: 1888

# BORDIGA
# VERMOUTH ROSSO

Distillery · Bordiga Liquori
Type · Vermouth

Bordiga's Vermouth Rosso is a jet-black drink inspired by the film noirs of the 1940s, with their dark tales of ruthless criminals and embittered detectives. Yet those references can surely only come from the drink's outward appearance because it certainly does not taste cynical. A little bitter perhaps, at most. "Typically Italian" would be an equally good way to describe this red vermouth, in which a subtle sweetness goes hand in hand with an abundance of Alpine herbs led by wormwood. Enjoy it neat, over ice with lemon, or as a base for a variety of classic cocktails. Bordiga produces vermouth in almost exactly the same way as it did in 1888, when the distillery first opened its doors in Cuneo in the mountains of Piedmont.

Alc/Vol: 18%
Location: Cuneo, Italy
Established: 1888

## MANCINO VERMOUTH VECCHIO

Distillery · La Canellesse
Type · Vermouth

Mancino rethinks the concept of vermouth, the traditional Italian aromatized wine, by aging their Rosso Amaranto in Italian oak barrels for a year. Vecchio is the first aged sweet vermouth, fragrant with oak and spice, and offering a deep, fruity nose with essences of cherry, honey, raisins, and dark chocolate. Bittersweet and slightly medicinal, the original vermouth is based on Trebbiano di Romagna white wine and sugar beet alcohol, and infused with almost 40 botanicals, including more esoteric ingredients like pimento, aloe, colombo spice, and quassia, in addition to the essential wormwood.

Alc/Vol: 42 %
Location: Piemont, Italy
Established: 1957

## VERMUT FALSET NEGRE

Distillery · Cooperativa Falset Marça
Type · Vermouth

Founded around a century ago, the two cooperatives located in the neighboring villages of Falset and Marça merged in 1999. The shared goal of the 500 partners was to make high-quality wine. They now produce 900,000 bottles each year using red and white grapes grown on vineyards covering 250 square meters of Tarragona countryside. It seems as if the cooperative values modesty quite highly, because it makes very little fuss about the brilliant reviews its products garner. The recipe for its deep-red Vermut Negre is nearly 100 years old and combines red Grenache Noir and Carignan grapes. The vermouth is aged for a year in wooden barrels and spends that time inhaling an infusion of 120 herbs. After some gentle sweetening, the ageing process continues for another three years.

Alc/Vol: 16 %
Location: Falset and Marça, Spain
Established: 1912

## VERMUT NEGRE

Distillery · Casa Mariol
Type · Vermouth

José María Vaquer founded the Casa Mariol wine brand in Batea in 1945. He clearly made a good impression as he toured Spain on sales tours in his Opel Blitz, because the whole country was soon talking about his wine. Miguel Angel Vaquer runs things these days along with his two siblings. A few years ago, he took over the Casa Mariol bar in Barcelona with the aim of getting people back into drinking vermouth. Vaquer is the kind of man who makes you eager to follow his recommendations, so presumably everyone who set foot in the bar tried the Vermut Negre. Based on white wine made from Macabeo grapes, the vermouth is darkened with green walnuts and flavored with numerous botanicals. At 11.5 %, it can be enjoyed with a lunchtime snack, just as tradition intended.

Alc/Vol: 11.5 %
Location: Batea, Spain
Established: 1945

# Casa Mariol

The Casa Mariol winery lies in the medieval village of Batea in the heart of Terra Alta in Catalonia. The Vaquer family have been running the estate for generations. Each of their wines is made from a single grape variety, which is unusual for Spain—but not for siblings Marta, Josep Maria, and Miquel Angel, who do a lot of things differently to the crowd. Their wines feature colorful labels with unpretentious lettering displayed at an avant-garde angle. Free of fussy flourishes and medals, they simply say what is in the bottle and use very few words to do so. The secret star of Casa Mariol is its vermouth, or vermú, as they say in Spain. Vermut Negre Casa Mariol comes in plain brown bottles that look as if they belong in a pharmacy, not a wine merchant. The glass is printed with white lettering that explains how to get the best out of your vermouth experience.

The liqueur is based on a wine made from Macabeo grapes and macerated with more than 100 botanicals. The recipe, which has remained unchanged for decades, pairs local herbs like rosemary and thyme with green walnuts, orange peel, wormwood, and cardamom. After spending six months in 60-year-old casks, the vermouth does its name very proud indeed. The taste is dark, velvety, bold, and intensely herbaceous. It is the perfect choice for the traditional hora del vermú (vermouth hour) that Miquel Angel Vaquer is reviving at his bar close to the Sagrada Familia in Barcelona. "Vermú," he says, "is a word that brings a smile to many older people's lips. It reminds them of their fondest memories, because the time when it was served was always the best time of the week."

## ATSBY
## AMBERTHORN VERMOUTH

Distillery · Rhys & Rylee
Type · Vermouth

The only reason Atsby founder Adam Ford finished his first—and average—vermouth was for the sake of his Italian girlfriend, who had first discovered the drink's herbal delights as a child. "The European vermouths stocking our bars were based on old recipes," says Ford. They were made using neutral alcohol and simple sweeteners. The main focus was on the effect of the botanicals. It was only on a trip to Italy that Ford learned how vermouth could really taste. He began working closely with a sommelier to produce an American take on the drink. Amberthorn is based on a New York chardonnay and an apple brandy from the Finger Lakes. The spices, which range from Chinese anise to French lavender, give the drink a gentle prickle that explains the thorn in its name.

Alc/Vol: 16 %
Location: New York (NY), USA
Established: 2012

## ATSBY
## ARMADILLO CAKE VERMOUTH

Distillery · Rhys & Rylee
Type · Vermouth

"Nothing requires more precision than making Vermouth," says Adam Ford of Atsby. Adding slightly too much of one ingredient can throw the whole drink out of balance. A common solution is to mask imperfections by adding more sweetener. Atsby's Armadillo Cake is definitely not sugary, though (if you discount the sweet-sounding name). Produced in small batches in New York, the vermouth uses caramel made from earthy, dark muscovado sugar from India. Alongside the ingredients you would expect from a red vermouth—such as cardamom and quassia—the recipe has some surprises in store, with wild celery, shitake, and nigella all making an appearance. The macabre story behind the name is probably better left untold. Suffice it to say that it involves an armadillo, a hood ornament, and a lot of blood.

Alc/Vol: 16 %
Location: New York (NY), USA
Established: 2012

## OSCAR.697
## ROSSO

Distillery · 697 srl
Type · Vermouth

Under the directorship of Stefano di Dio, OSCAR.697 assembles the expertise of three diverse craftsmen to create a traditional Italian vermouth that is also eminently modern. The Roman-born bartender Oscar Quagliarini perfected a recipe of all-natural ingredients for this sweet red vermouth, still drier and more bitter than the norm at 14% sugar content, with notes of absinthe, rhubarb, and liquorice. Manufactured in Asti at La Canellese, the final result is captured in a sanded glass bottle designed by David Caon, the label giving prominence to the exacting process and plum-colored liquid.

Alc/Vol: 16%
Location: Milan, Italy
Established since: 2012

## OSCAR.697
## BIANCO

Distillery · 697 srl
Type · Vermouth

Following the success of their n°697 Rosso, Milan's OSCAR.697 has released a sweet white vermouth, perfect for cocktails like the Negroni or Manhattan or served shaken with ice. The n°773 Bianco, following a secret recipe by mixologist Oscar Quagliarini, combines delicate flavors of bergamot, yarrow muscat, and elderflower, adhering to a tradition 150 years in the making. Like all of OSCAR.697's products, it is made with natural ingredients, most of them certified organic, in the Piedmont village of Calamandra, where Oreste Sconfienza has made vermouth for over 50 years at La Canellese.

Alc/Vol: 16%
Location: Milan, Italy
Established since: 2012

# MERWUT

### Distillery · Dorst & Consorten
### Type · Vermouth

Dorst & Consorten have a reputation for innovative and "non-conformist" wines, from dry rieslings to defined pinot noirs based on the long-standing viniculture tradition in the Palatinate. Most recently, they have experimented with wormwood, infusing the bitter, digestive herb in German white wine and brandy to produce their Merwut. The palate balances spicy, sweet, and bitter tones, preserving the singular taste of wormwood in contrast to the subdued flavors of commercial vermouths. The gradual growth of annual production to 1,500 bottles enables an attentive devotion to the process.

Alc/Vol: 18 %
Location: Landau, Germany
Established: 2010

# SEASONAL WILDFLOWER

### Distillery · Uncouth Vermouth
### Type · Vermouth

Bianca Miraglia, a young entrepreneur living in Brooklyn, is totally committed to sustainability and seasonality. Her Uncouth Vermouths are based on ingredients that do not follow market forces but instead grow naturally around Brooklyn or are supplied by local farmers. The base wine comes from nearby vineyards, and Miraglia uses no added flavorings, sugar, or sweeteners. Although she does not import any ingredients from faraway places, her Wildflower vermouth features the kind of intense floral bouquet that you would not necessarily expect to get from Brooklyn.

Alc/Vol: 17 %
Location: Brooklyn (NY), USA
Established: 2012

# Uncouth Vermouth

The logo that adorns the bottles of Uncouth Vermouth shows a woman prudently and defiantly sticking her finger up her nose. Bianca Miraglia (30), New York's youngest maker of vermouth and the owner of Uncouth, very much sees herself as following in the tradition of European vermouth. She makes her aperitif using common wormwood (Artemisia vulgaris) and attaches a great deal of importance to achieving dry, bitter notes. This puts her well and truly in line with American and even European regulations. Things are pretty simple in the United States, where vermouth simply has to taste like vermouth. In Europe, the drink must contain an extract of one of the many varieties of the Artemisia genus.

Italian producers, however, would probably strongly deny that this counts as vermouth. They would say that Miraglia is far too unconventional in the way she selects her other ingredients. She freely mixes small and tiny batches of herbs and juices with regional wine and brandy, and takes a strictly seasonal approach to her work. Miraglia forages herbs from the countryside or picks them in her mother's garden. Other ingredients come from local farmers. Anything that is not currently growing does not get used. The drink is neither sweetened nor filtered.

Her philosophy produces aperitifs that are extremely distinctive, headstrong, and charming. The very dry apple-mint vermouth and the spicy, floral mix of lavender and serrano chili demand to be explored and enjoyed by those with an intrepid palate. The only extras you will need are an ice cube and an adventurous spirit.

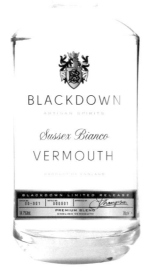

## LACKDOWN
## SUSSEX BIANCO VERMOUTH

Distillery · Blackdown Distillery
Type · Vermouth

Blackdown Silver Sussex Bianco Vermouth is the first white vermouth produced in England, produced amid the chalk hills of the South Downs. The birch trees surrounding the Lurgashall Winery are tapped in early spring, and the sap is fortified and infused with a carefully guarded blend of locally-grown herbs and spices in small handmade batches. The pale golden liquid has a creamy flavor, with notes of wormwood, chamomile, and juniper encapsulating the taste of the English countryside. It can be savored on its own as an aperitif or paired with Sussex Dry Gin in a new take on the dry martini.

Alc/Vol: 14.7 %
Location: West Sussex, United Kingdom
Established: 2013

## BELSAZAR
## VERMOUTH DRY

Distillery · Alfred Schladerer
Alte Schwarzwälder Hausbrennerei
Type · Vermouth

Belsazar Vermouth is based on South Baden wines, Schladerer fruit brandy, and a careful selection of herbs, blending the unique flavor of wormwood and other notes with the rich sweetness of the regional grapes. The ingredients form a harmonious mixture in stoneware containers to avoid any cask aftertaste. The dry, red, rosé, and white varieties each offer a distinct palate, from delicate apricot and chamomile to notes of candied orange peel and bitter chocolate, from summery pink grapefruit and currants to fiery pomeranze and cinchona bark, with the characteristic bittersweet aftertaste.

Alc/Vol: 19 %
Location: Staufen im Breisgau, Germany
Established: 1844

# The Best Medicine

•

In the monasteries and apothecaries of the Middle Ages, herbs, spices, roots, and petals were mixed, chopped, dried, finely grated, and preserved in alcohol. To reduce the bitterness of the medicinal herbal mixtures, a syrup would often be added or they would be aged in wood barrels. Little wonder, then, that people soon started serving these digestifs after every large meal.

# Borgmann 1772

Germany's digestif culture is pretty antiquated and dusty as far as its herbal liqueurs go (despite one particular brand being a huge export success). A few years ago, though, three friends from Brunswick and Berlin started proving that it does not have to be that way. Jan Borgmann, who lives in Brunswick, runs a traditional German pharmacy in which a recipe for a homemade herbal liqueur is passed from one manager to the next. Jan's brother Hendrik and their friend Jörn Clausen live in Berlin and found that whenever they took the digestif to parties, it would prove really popular. "In 2006, we decided to bring the product up-to-date and combine tradition, design, and quality," says Clausen. The 1772 in the name refers to the year that August Wilhelm, Duke of Brunswick-Wolfenbüttel, gave the pharmacy privileged status by naming it a court apothecary. Borgmann 1772 is still partially produced in the pharmacy and comes in a stylish aluminum-coated bottled. The trio also have their designer friends come up with fresh new looks for each limited edition they produce. The latest addition to their business is a café, which is located right by the pharmacy in Brunswick. It has coffee, snacks, and (of course) Borgmann 1772. Drinkers can enjoy it as a classic digestif, served either chilled or at room temperature. Alternatively, they can go for something a little bit different, such as a Borgmann Tonic, a Borgmann Sour, and even a Singapore Sling with Borgmann. In short, these three guys are doing a great job at dusting off the humble German herbal liqueur.

## BORGMANN 1772
## EDITION NO 9 GESTALTEN

Distillery · Borgmann & Clausen
Type · Herbal liqueurs

If the world's most popular herbal liqueur is made just outside the town where you live, you might end up thinking that you should have a go at making your own. That is exactly what happened with Jan and Hendrik Borgmann. At the time, their parents were running a pharmacy in Brunswick that had been in the family for generations. This meant Jan and Hendrik had access to raw materials, a laboratory, and the necessary knowledge. Along with their friend Jörg Clausen, they revived an old family recipe that had been passed down through the generations by word of mouth. They bottled the liqueur in stylish metal bottles and took it to Berlin, where it became established in no time at all. Today, Borgmann 1772 is available throughout Germany.

## KRÄUTERELIXIER

Distillery · Gebrüder Elwert
Type · Herbal liqueurs

The Elwert family tradition of distillation does not originate in a mere pastime, but in fact grew out of the apothecary, where spirits and herbal infusions were used for medicinal purposes. Their new creation is Gyld, an herbal elixir inspired by the magic potions of invincibility described in ancient sagas. Carefully infused for months, the liqueur has a mild taste that blends local herbs with oriental specimens for a complex flavor. The form and design of the bottle evokes the traditional pharmacist's vessels while emphasizing the bright yellow-gold color, whose origin is kept secret.

## PIJÖKEL 55

Distillery ·
Grote Spirituosen Manufaktur
Type · Herbal liqueurs

In the vernacular of Northern Germany, "Pijökel" refers to a small object. One day in Bremen in 1955, it was also used to christen a scrap of burl wood by a group of friends, including future pharmacist Kuno Grote. He would go on to develop the singular liqueur named after this formative event, beginning in his apothecary and now made by a second generation in the center of Berlin. The unique, spicy spirit is redolent with clove, cinnamon, ginger, and other botanicals—a bittersweet digestive following the secret original recipe, bottled by hand in long-necked, matte black glass bottles.

---

Alc/Vol: 39%
Location: Brunswick, Germany
Established: 1772

Alc/Vol: 34%
Location: Böhmenkirch, Germany
Established: 2013

Alc/Vol: 42.5%
Location: Berlin, Germany
Established: 2010

## BËSK

Distillery · Letherbee Distillers
Type · Herbal liqueurs

Bësk is Letherbee Distillers' take on malört, an esoteric but infamous Swedish liqueur based on wormwood: Letherbee's version, from a recipe by Robert Haynes, is a sophisticated rendition in which the bitterness of wormwood is matched with notes of grapefruit, earthy gentian root, star anise, and elderflower musk. Haynes convinced Brenton Engel to make a limited run of the liqueur in his distillery, based in an industrial building in Chicago's Ravenswood neighborhood. Though it remains a challenging drink both on its own and as a cocktail ingredient, Bësk has become one of Letherbee's staples.

Alc/Vol: 50 %
Location: Chicago (IL), USA
Established: 2012

## GINGER CAT
## ORGANIC LIQUEUR

Distillery · Brennerei Ehringhausen
Type · Herbal liqueurs

Every mom has a recipe that makes her the undefeated expert for that particular dish, cake, cookie, etc. And no matter how closely you stick to the quantities and the method, you will never be able to achieve the same result. Till Bohn is an exception to that rule. His mother's home-steeped ginger liqueur meant that her dining table was a veritable (and much-frequented) place of pilgrimage for her guests. Till wanted to find a way of letting the rest of the world share in the experience. By teaming up with the family-run Ehringhausen distillery in Werne, he was able to make that dream come true. Ginger Cat (30%) is made with a 12-year-old, barrel-aged wine spirit flavored with ginger, which makes it pleasantly spicy, and acacia honey, which adds a sweetish note to the all-organic liqueur.

Alc/Vol: 30 %
Location: Cologne, Germany
Established: 2012

## HOPKA

Distillery · Indio Spirits
Type · Herbal liqueurs

The three men who make up the team behind Indio Spirits are American archetypes, guys who look like they just stepped out of a Tom Wolfe novel. The chairman and distiller are both broad-shouldered, robust, and rarely without a baseball cap, while the president is an older bon vivant. Their drinks, however, most certainly do not conform to type. John Ufford, the founder of the brand, has always given his vodkas a twist with ingredients like blackberry, wasabi, and lemongrass. The brand's gin, rum, and, most recently, whiskey creations are also built on the back of experiments. The latest project is Hopka, a hop liqueur made of grain alcohol with Cascade and Citra hops from the fertile Willamette Valley that borders Portland to the south. Hopka has been made for craft beer enthusiasts and can be treated like vodka, gin, or whiskey.

Alc/Vol: 40 %
Location: Portland (OR), USA
Established: 2004

## FERNET LEOPOLD
## HIGHLAND AMARO

Distillery · Leopold Bros.
Type · Herbal liqueurs

After graduating high school, Todd and Scott Leopold left Colorado to continue their education. Todd earned a diploma in brewing and then headed to Munich to build on his knowledge there. Scott, meanwhile, earned degrees in industrial and environmental engineering. They came together again in Michigan, where they combined their respective talents and founded Leopold Bros. brewery in 1999. Not long after that, they added a distillery. Ever since then—and now in their new location in their hometown of Denver—the brothers have been producing celebrated organic spirits such as absinthe and vodka. Their award-winning Fernet Leopold Highland Amaro (40%) has a pronounced, highly unusual mint quality that blends in perfectly with bitter roots and a bouquet of chamomile, honeysuckle, elderflower, and rose petals.

Alc/Vol: 40%
Location: Denver (CO), USA
Established: 1999

## BIGALLET VIRIANA
## CHINA-CHINA

Distillery · Bigallet
Type · Bitter liqueur

Félix von Bigallet opened a syrup and liqueur factory in Lyon in 1872. Once it was up and running, he packed a few samples into his carriage and set off to promote them around France. Among the liqueurs was Viriana China China, a digestif made by macerating and distilling sweet and bitter orange peels. Other ingredients include citrus blossom, oranges, cinchona, and a secret blend of herbs. The drink gets its dark color from caramelized sugar. Legend has it that a liqueur manufacturer from Isère became so enchanted by one of his assistants, the beautiful China China, that he forgot about the sugar he was heating. It ended up burning, which produced the caramel flavor that would later prove so popular.

Alc/Vol: 40%
Location: Virieu-sur-Bourbre, France
Established: 1872

# Leopold Bros.

When the U.S. authorities finally lifted the country's long-standing ban on absinthe in 2007, Todd Leopold did not wait long to start making it. At the time, Todd, a trained beer brewer, was running a small brewpub in Ann Arbor, Michigan, with his brother Scott. Business was going well, thanks to Todd having learned his craft. He holds a diploma from the Siebel Institute in Chicago and trained in Germany, the home of beer brewing, at Würzburger Hofbräu in Würzburg and Fässla in Bamberg. Since Scott and Todd were only permitted to sell alcohol that they had manufactured, Todd began experimenting with distilling spirits: "We started with vodka and gin, and immediately followed that with our many liqueurs. We needed to fill our bar so that we could make cocktails," says Todd, now the master distiller at Leopold Bros. When, in 2008, the brewery's new owner declined to extend the lease on the building, the brothers used it as an opportunity to return to their hometown of Denver, Colorado.

They sold their brewing equipment and concentrated on distilling. It proved to be the right decision. With demand for handcrafted spirits booming in the U.S., Leopold Bros. quickly earned a very good name for itself. The brothers make 20 spirits and liqueurs in total. They cover gin, whiskey, and everything in between. A particular highlight is their Absinthe Verte, which uses imported Chilean pisco as a base for the traditional ingredients of anise, fennel, and wormwood. "The spirit is clear at first, so we heat it to 120 degrees and add hyssop, petit wormwood, and lemon balm. The warm alcohol pulls the chlorophyll out of the botanicals, which lends the absinthe its pretty green color," says Todd, explaining the production process. Visitors to the new factory that the brothers have recently opened can watch all the spirits being made live. One of the best parts of the tour is getting a glimpse into the area where Todd and a few helpers malt the barley for the whiskey. It is extremely rare for this step to happen in the distillery itself.

# Amaro

•

**Federico Fellini's *La Dolce Vita* is a celluloid monument to the Italian way of life. Ever since it hit our screens, "the sweet life" has evoked a worldwide longing for Italy. Its sweetness goes down especially well with a bitter liqueur known as amaro.**

When Federico Fellini brought *La Dolce Vita* to cinema screens in 1960, he was hoping it would encourage Italy's superficial jet set to take a long, hard look at itself. But the pulsating nightlife on the Via Veneto in Rome did not end up becoming a symbol of Italy's decadent upper classes—instead, the film made the street a desirable destination for rich, beautiful people the world over. Ever since then, the Italians have been considered experts in letting their hair down and enjoying the sweet things in life over a good meal. Not everything about that meal has to taste sweet, though, as a look at Italy's many varieties of amaro shows. Commonly drunk as a digestif after dinner, the herbal liqueurs are now also used in cocktails and long drinks, and have won themselves a permanent place in bar culture.

"Amaro" means "bitter" in Italian. The name is a reminder of the fact that the drink was originally intended for use as a medicine, not as something to enjoy. Italian monks believed that by mixing herbs from their monastery garden with alcohol, they could preserve their effects and thereby ward off illness and even the devil himself. They based their liqueurs on distillates that were more alcoholic than wine or beer. The amaro got its flavor from the herbs that were added. Although the medicine went into industrial production in the nineteenth century, the way it was made never changed. To this day, an amaro still contains between 15% and 39% alcohol, which means it will keep for a particularly long time. Up to 60 different herbs are added to the drink—the details of which are, of course, a tightly guarded secret. Amari differ according to region, so if you find yourself traveling through Italy, it is well worth avoiding the usual Ramazzotti and asking about local distilleries instead.

While amaro is mostly drunk as a digestif in Italy, mixologists in other countries take a more creative approach to the liqueur. "If you think that amaro should be used in small quantities like other herbal liqueurs, then you've misunderstood the drink. I use amaro as the basis for a lot of my cocktails. Why not?" says Chaim Dauermann, who used to be the bar manager at New York's 'inoteca. He explains that, after years of drinking Aperol Spritz and other

sweet drinks, many of his guests are looking to experience more diverse tastes. "Amaro is sophisticated and complicated," says the team from Brovospirits in Washington. "At it's best, it is a sensory journey." Brovospirits recently put a whole new spin on amaro's tradition of regional connections: "We asked seven local bartenders if they wanted to make amaro with us. We thought one or two would say yes, but all seven said yes." And so Project Amaro ended up making seven very different amari because "each city balances bitter and sweet in very different ways." The fact that amaro has made itself a permanent feature of so many bar shelves in recent years is surely down to its diversity—no amaro ever tastes the same as the next.

Yet all trends and enthusiasm for experiments aside, the long-standing belief in amaro's medicinal properties is probably one of the reasons why the drink is such a matter of course in its native country. Many Italian physicians go against the scientific evidence and recommend regular consumption of amaro to prevent indigestion. It is also said that having a full stomach can put a person in a bad mood. This is why Italians do not attach much importance to conversations held during business meals. Only once you have digested everything are you considered to have regained full possession of your mental capacities. So there could, in fact, be a glimmer of truth to the rumor that a nip or two of amaro can help keep the devil at bay.

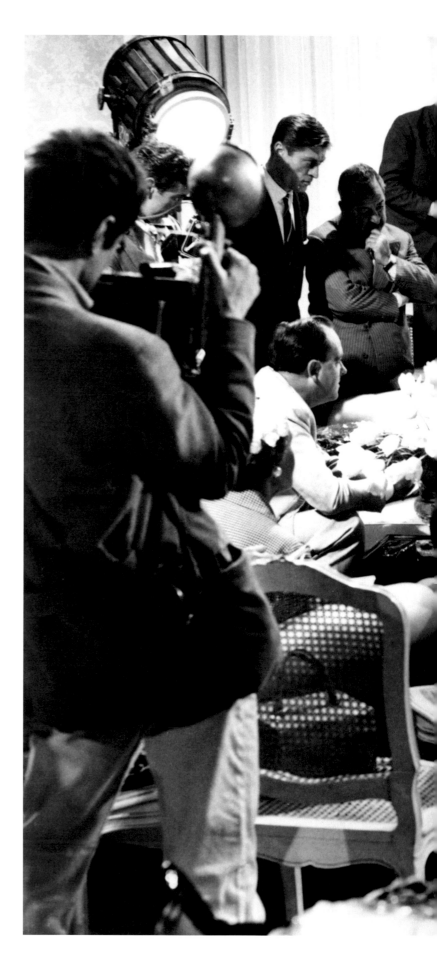

## GRAN CLASSICO BITTER

Distillery · Erlebnisbrennerei Kallnach

Type · Amaro

The original "Turin Bitter" recipe dates back to 1864, a classic preparation of various herbs and roots, including the essential wormwood, with no additional flavor or color. In 1925, the recipe was purchased and brought to Switzerland, where it has been produced by the Kallnach distillery ever since. A multifaceted, bittersweet concoction, the maceration of bitter orange peel, rhubarb, and other ingredients imbues the liquid with a golden amber hue. Gran Classico Bitter can be served on ice, with soda water, or in place of standard red bitters in any cocktail for a more complex result.

## THE BITTER TRUTH E\*\*X\*\*R

Distillery · Dolin for The Bitter Truth

Type · Bitter liqueur

Since 2006, The Bitter Truth has been dedicated to the renaissance of bitters as a crucial cocktail component. Munich bartenders Stephan Berg and Alexander Hauck recognized the lack of high-quality bitters and the complete disappearance of some historical strains, and sought to revive both classics and obscure traditions. E\*\*X\*\*R references the medicinal origins of the drink: the dark herbal bitter liqueur evokes the flavors of dark chocolate, coffee and caramel, and Alpine herbs. It works as well in northern versions of the classic Manhattan or Negroni as it does on its own as a digestif.

## MONDINO AMARO

Distillery · Brennerei Schnitzer

Type · Bitter liqueur

Mondino, an Italian-inspired aperitif, reflects the rich intersection of Italian and German culture in the foothills of the Bavarian Alps. Distiller Hans Schnitzer brought the idea over the Alps in the 1960s after his apprenticeship, and perfected the recipe over generations using local fruit and aromatic herbs. Half a century later, his grandson Max rediscovered this family specialty, and the two collaborated to recreate it. Updated with the techniques of modern craftsmanship, Mondino transforms organic bitter orange, rhubarb, yellow gentian, and other ingredients into this versatile cordial.

---

Alc/Vol: 28 %
Location: Kallnach, Schweiz
Established: 1925

Alc/Vol: 30 %
Location: Chambéry, France
Established: 2006

Alc/Vol: 18 %
Location: Traunstein, Germany
Established: 2013

## LIQUORE DI GENEPY

Distillery · Pàlent
Type · Bitter liqueur

After leading a professional life during Italy's post-war economic boom, Matteo Laugero dedicated himself to reviving the agricultural tradition in his native Palènt, a small village in the upper Valle Maira. His family practices biodynamic cultivation of genepy, an Alpine wormwood, with rustic spring water irrigation channels coursing through the steep fields and brambles of their estate. In a small workshop in San Damiano Macra, Laugero and his two sons infuse the plant in organic wheat alcohol and bottle on-site, producing a fragrant spirit faithful to the ancient traditions of the valley.

Alc/Vol: 38%
Location: San Damiano Macra, Italy
Established: 2002

# Palènt

Palènt, a hamlet surrounded by beech and pine forests, lies 1,500 meters above sea level in Piedmont's Maira Valley. Matteo Laugero was born here, but later left to make a living in the stationary business. As the years went by, he decided he had had enough of being a shopkeeper and, once his children had flown the nest, he moved back up into the mountains. This was not, however, about living a life of solitude, but about starting a new career as a distiller.

Genepy, a plant related to wormwood and the main ingredient in the spirit he was planning to make, grows wild at high altitudes in the Piedmont Alps. It is particularly fond of making its home on scree and in hard-to-reach cracks in the cliffs. A few of the plants had started growing around Laugero's unoccupied childhood home. It was almost as if they had gathered there to try and nudge him in the right direction. He took the hint and,

using an irrigation system and pure spring water, increased the number of plants until he had more than 40,000 of them. He even managed to persuade them to arrange themselves into neat and tidy rows. Cultivating the plants like this involves a lot of manual labor. Laugero and his two sons have to collect the seeds, re-sow them, and look after the plants until they mature. It takes three years for the genepy to go from seed to glass. Cold maceration is used to get the intense flavor from the plants into the alcohol, which is made from organic wheat. The post-distillation result is a mildly sweet, oily, and extremely aromatic herbal liqueur that is a welcome guest in Turin's finest restaurants. You can also enjoy the fruits of Laugero's labor at the Palènt alpine lodge, where his wife Virginia serves the 38% genepy alongside delicious Italian delicacies.

# Mixers

•

Long drinks and cocktails would be nothing without them,
but the most popular mixers — tonic water, ginger beer, bitter
lemon — generally taste pretty synthetic. Drinks experts
think it is time this changed and have started tinkering with
traditional recipes.

Mixers make a short drink long and bring a welcome twist of freshness to a cocktail. But the most popular among them—tonic water, ginger beer, and bitter lemon—generally taste pretty synthetic. Drinks experts think it is time this changed and have started tinkering with traditional recipes. Whoever first decided to mix their wine with club soda must have had the idea very soon after Joseph Priestley invented the carbonated water in Leeds in 1772. We know this because spritzers had become a fixture of polite European society by the end of the eighteenth century. Not long after that, the first flavored sodas hit the shelves. "The first tonic water was created by Erasmus Bond in 1858 and manufactured by W. Pitt & Co. in London," says Tristan Donovan, author of a comprehensive guide to soda entitled *Fizz: How Soda Shook up the World.* "It was billed as a way to stop malaria and had a huge amount of quinine in it, which gave it a very bitter taste. To overcome the bitterness, British troops in India would mix it with gin. That's what gave rise to the Gin & Tonic," he explains. Schweppes launched its Indian Tonic Water in 1870 and began supplying it to the British army.

Mixers became extremely popular in Prohibition America, partly because they were good at camouflaging alcohol and partly because the moonshine people were making was too strong to drink neat.

Now, nearly a century later, drinks connoisseurs are facing a very different problem: if people are placing increasing value on the quality of gin, vodka, and the like, then why are they still being mixed with bog-standard, industrially produced soft drinks? The ratio of alcohol to mixer in a long drink can be as much as 1:3. "It's kind of like spending hours expertly cooking a piece of Kobe beef on a low heat and then smothering it in ketchup," laughs Peter Hundert who, along with Hendrik Schaulin, runs a company in Hamburg that makes tonic and ginger syrups from all-natural ingredients. The syrups can be mixed with fizzy water to make the drink as strong or as weak as you like. While this approach is too time consuming for professional bartenders, people like to use it at home as a way of wowing their guests. Hundert, a photographer, and Schaulin, a stylist, started their syrup kitchen as an experiment, but the products proved so popular that the hobby has now grown into a small business called pHenomenal.

As for the bars, Schweppes long had what essentially amounted to a monopoly on the mixers that they stocked. However, it is now becoming increasingly common to see other names adorning the little glass bottles. Fever Tree, Thomas Henry, Goldberg, and Fentimans are just a few of the many tonic brands that are enriching today's bar culture. From sweet to extra-bitter, small bubbles to large, and flavored with thyme or rosemary, modern tonics are being designed with as much care and attention as the spirits for which they are intended. What is more, the recipes for ginger beer, lemonade, and cola are also being shaken up. Long drinks, it seems, will never be the same again.

# Craft Spirits & Craft Cocktails

•

**Legendary bartender Jim Meehan talks about using craft spirits in his bar, the cocktail renaissance, and passionate cocktail drinkers.**

Jim Meehan has made history with his 20-seater New York bar, Please Don't Tell. The bar, which serves excellent drinks and is accessed through a door behind a phone box in a hot dog store, set a global trend in motion a few years back. Speakeasies, hidden bars of the kind that sprang up during America's prohibition period, can now be found in backrooms and basements in every fashionable city in the world. This has made Meehan a legend in the bar scene. The quality of the cocktails on offer at Please Don't Tell (a.k.a. PDT) has helped it win over everyone who walks through the door. But Meehan says the guests themselves and a good atmosphere are the secret to a bar's success. He also places a lot of importance on individuality—in his choice of spirits, in the cocktails he creates, and in his interactions with guests.

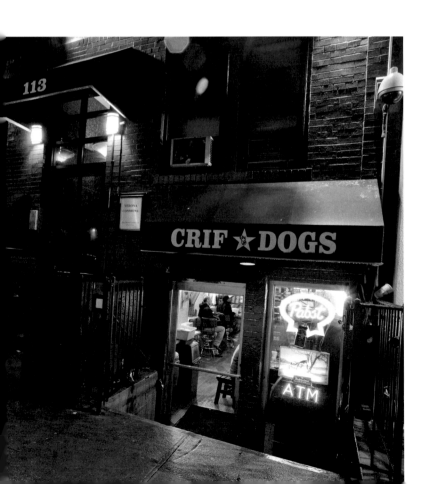

**Let's start with a basic question: Do you have any craft spirits on the menu of PDT?**

Of course! Right now, we're pouring Clear Creek Kirschwasser, Pear & Plum Brandy, Woody Creek Vodka, Mr. Katz's Rock & Rye, and Barr Hill Tom Cat Gin. And that's just domestic "craft" spirits. These spirits are in 6 of our 18 cocktails. Ultimately, we use them because they're delicious! All of these distillers are friends or acquaintances of mine, which is motivation to support them; but at the end of the day, the quality of their products is why we mix with them.

**Does the rise of the craft spirits affect and change your work as a bartender?**

Absolutely. As a buyer for a bar, it's my job to taste as much as I can to bring in the best ingredients for our cocktails and products for our customers. With hundreds of new distilleries, this means I must taste more often and make important decisions with very little reference material to validate or nullify my decision. Oftentimes, (thankfully) I'm one of the first people to taste new products. It's an honor. Sometimes I'm right about a product, but occasionally I feel like I made the wrong decision.

**What would you say is the most meaningful difference between an artisan spirit and a standard product?**

While mass-produced spirits like Absolut Vodka, Maker's Mark Bourbon, Johnny Walker Scotch Whisky, Tanqueray Gin or Remy Martin Cognac (I could go on) are certainly not artisan, they're quality benchmarks within their categories. This being said, artisan spirits are typically more idiosyncratic than the big brands: they bear the mark of their maker, tend to vary in character from batch to batch, and often subvert category conventions. Standard products are consistent in quality and character year after year: something I value as a mixologist.

**Do you find a difference in how craft spirits taste compared to their more industrial "relatives"?**

For me, commercial production is industrial by nature and taste is entirely subjective. The larger a company, the easier it is for them to keep their costs down. For this reason, bigger companies can afford to age their spirits longer, utilize more consistent production methods, and afford more elaborate packaging. Smaller brands pay more to produce. In order to remain competitive, craft producers must overcome the financial hurdles with thoughtful products that not only taste great; they channel the popular zeitgeist. Small ships can maneuver better than the big ones, but watch out when the big ones are headed in the right direction.

**Does the cocktail renaissance have something to do with the rise of craft distilleries. Or vice versa?**

Yes and no. Certain craft distillers like Lance Winters, Marko Karakasevic, Todd Leopold, and Ralph Erenzo have been around as long or longer than the modern cocktail renaissance. Neither movement would exist without passionate consumers, and it just so happens that most people who value artisanal spirits appreciate craft cocktails. Most consumers at high-end cocktail bars prefer to drink local if possible, and for this reason, craft distillers and bartenders are working more closely than they did in the past. Collaborations between distillers and bartenders, including brands created and owned by bartenders, is an exciting new trend in the craft space.

234

**As a guest in a bar, do you expect to find craft spirits on the menu?**

Depends on the bar. If I see local beer, wine, and food on the menu, I tend to look for local spirits. This being said, there are many markets around the world where distilling is prohibitively expensive due to government regulations or competitive trade relations, so spirits lag behind other local specialties.

**When you travel, are local distilleries something you look out for?**

They are! I'm fascinated by spirits production.

**Would you share a recipe for a cocktail based on a craft spirit?**

Afternine:

| | |
|---|---|
| 8 oz | lavender mint tea, freshly brewed |
| 1 oz | Monkey 47 Schwarzwald Dry Gin |
| 0.5 oz | Marie Brizard White Crème de Cacao |
| 0.25 oz | Green Chartreuse V.E.P. |

Build in a pre-warmed insulated mug
Garnish with a sprig of mint and lavender

# Index

About the authors

## Cathrin Brandes

Cathrin Brandes is a gastronomy consultant and author. Her annual food trend reports are widely quoted and highly trusted. For her, drinking, reviewing, and writing about good spirits is far more than just an important part of her profession; it is her passion.

Texts: 29, 30–33, 35, 42–45, 56–59, 62, 76–79, 82, 124, 128, 132, 135, 138–143, 146, 149, 171, 182–187, 196–199, 202, 207, 230–235

## The Weekender

Since 2011, Christian Schneider and Dirk Mönkemöller have been publishing the German magazine The Weekender, which comes out four times a year under the subtitle „Magazin für Einblicke und Ausflüge" (Magazine for Insights and Outings). The prize-winning magazine focuses on themes like living, travel, food, and nature.

Texts: 18, 47, 95, 175, 176, 212, 217

## Christoph Keller

Christoph Keller is one of the most sought-after distillers in the world. At Stählemühle, his distillery on Lake Constance, he produces small batches of exceptional spirits using orchard and wild fruit, herbs, spices, mushrooms, and nuts. He is also the master distiller for Monkey 47 Schwarzwald Dry Gin.

Texts: 8–12, 160–163

# Index

# Index

# Index

# Out of the Jar
## the Jar

## Crafted Spirits & Liqueurs

This book was conceived, edited, and designed by Gestalten.

Edited by Cathrin Brandes, Christian Schneider,
Dirk Mönkemöller, and Robert Klanten

Features and portraits: Cathrin Brandes, Dirk Mönkemöller, and
Anna Lea Pasdzierny
Features on Gin and Distillation: Christoph Keller
Product descriptions: Anna Lea Pasdzierny and Thomas Domenig
Translation from the German: Jen Metcalf
Product descriptions originally in English: Tamar Shafrir
Proofreading: Felix Lennert

Cover image: Stählemühle by Albrecht Fuchs
Back cover images: Glendalough Distillery by Bárbara Crepaldi;
Gin Sul by Stephan Garbe; Chase Distillery

Creative direction by Christian Schneider and Dirk Mönkemöller
Layout by Moya Ehlers and Jeannine Moser
Typeface: Buenos Aires by Luzi Gantenbein

Printed by Nino Druck GmbH, Neustadt / Weinstraße
Made in Germany

Published by Gestalten, Berlin 2015
ISBN 978-3-89955-571-4

For more information, please visit www.gestalten.com.

Bibliographic information published by the Deutsche Nationalbibliothek:
The Deutsche Nationalbibliothek lists this publication in the Deutsche Nationalbibliografie;
detailed bibliographic data are available online at
http://dnb.d-nb.de.

None of the content in this book was published in exchange for payment by commercial parties
or designers; Gestalten selected all included work based solely on its artistic merit.

This book was printed on paper certified according to the standards of the FSC®.